THE ESL WONDER WORKBOOK # 2

ALL AROUND ME

A Book of Lessons and Seatwork
For New Students of English

Elizabeth Claire

✧

With illustrations by
J. D. Frazier

✧

Original turtle designs
by Yi Lo Cheng

Also available from Alta Book Company

THE ESL WONDER WORKBOOK #1:

THIS IS ME

by Elizabeth Claire

Edited by Charles Marden Chapman

Alta Book Company, Publishers - San Francisco
16 Adrian Court, Burlingame, California, 94010, USA

Illustrations and typesetting by J.D. Frazier, Santa Barbara, California

ISBN 1-878598-01-5

TABLE OF CONTENTS

Acknowledgements

This book owes its existence to the new students and their mainstream teachers at School Number Two in Fort Lee, New Jersey who clamored for simple, do-able ESL activities to insure the productive and effective use of their time.

A special thanks to Terri Lehmann for a careful reading of the first draft of the teacher's instructions. I also want to acknowledge the expert editing on the manuscript by Charles Marden Chapman and his steadfast support throughout the production of the book.

Thanks to Mark Lieberman for his example of professional discipline, his editorial assistance, and his homemade soup.

The turtle characters were created in 1986 by Yi Lo Cheng, then age 10. Several of the illustrations are based on the originals by this prize-winning young artist from Taiwan. These have been adapted and artfully executed by Joe Frazier, whom I thank for his own delightful illustrations as well as the design and typesetting of the ESL WONDER WORKBOOKS 1 & 2.

About the author

Elizabeth Claire graduated magna cum laude from the City College of New York and was elected into Phi Beta Kappa. She received the Downer Medal of Excellence for Hispanic Studies and was awarded an Experienced Teacher's Fellowship to New York University where she received her Master's Degree in Teaching English as a Second Language. She has taught ESL for the past twenty years to students of all ages and backgrounds. A resident of Saddle Brook, New Jersey, she is the author of nine other books.

Other works for ESL students and their teachers by Ms. Claire:

ESL Wonder Workbook #1: This Is Me

ESL Teacher's Activities Kit

ESL Teacher's Holiday Activities Kit

Three Little Words: A, An, and The: A Foreign Student's Guide to English Articles

Hi! English for Children

What's So Funny? A Foreign Student's Guide to American Humor

Just-a-Minute! An Oral Language-learning Game

An Indispensible Guide to Dangerous English!

Health Care Choices

About this book

THE ESL WONDER WORKBOOKS fill the need for plentiful seatwork to reinforce oral lessons for young beginning students of English. THE ESL WONDER WORKBOOK #2: ALL AROUND ME continues building basic vocabulary and useful sentence structures. It is best used following THE ESL WONDER WORKBOOK #1: THIS IS ME, but it will also stand on its own. The simple reading, writing, matching, drawing, coloring and other activities insure the productive use of the newly arrived child's time, and are especially useful in helping to integrate in mainstream classes students who cannot understand or participate in classroom work. Each page of THE ESL WONDER WORKBOOKS focuses on a single, immediately useful language concept with limited vocabulary, leading to easy comprehension and success.

THE ESL WONDER WORKBOOK #2: ALL AROUND ME concentrates at first on survival English. Terms for street safety, school rules and activities, colors, lunch room vocabulary, numbers, money, clothing, calendar, time and weather are all presented in non-cumulative, basic entry-level units. Basic language is also given for playing games, making friends and paying compliments. Grammatical contrasts are presented for observation and discovery, rather than through rules. The final pages on animals incorporate practice with verbs, adjectives, prepositions and common present tense sentence structures, but the emphasis is always on the content, not on the grammar. At the end of THE ESL WONDER WORKBOOK #2: ALL AROUND ME, students will be able to write a short composition describing a favorite animal, and a composition about themselves, their abilities, preferences, and appearance.

To the teacher: how to use this book

The objectives and simple procedures for each lesson are given on each student page. These and the following suggestions will help teachers, especially mainstream classroom teachers without specific ESL training, make each lesson a success for both student and instructor.

1. Give the new student meaningful work to do the first day he or she arrives in your class. If the student is not able to participate in the mainstream class (which could be several hours a day for the first few months), provide for his or her instruction using THE ESL WONDER WORKBOOKS. Other materials helpful for the student include:

a) a picture dictionary.

b) a bilingual dictionary with both English-native language and native language-English sections.

c) classroom textbooks for the ESL student to browse through.

d) a battery-operated tape recorder with headphones.

2. There must be language input, in order to achieve the instructional benefits. There should be interaction with English speakers both before and after the pages are complete. The aim is for the student to mentally practice the new words and sentences as he or she is coloring or writing on a page.

3. Help the student connect words with meanings. Speak slowly and clearly; use real objects, actions, facial expression and gestures as well as the pictures to insure that the student understands the new words and structures.

4. Do not translate the instructions. The student will easily learn to follow instructions in English. Mime the actions, holding a pencil, crayon, scissors or whatever is needed and point to the place where the student is to write, draw, cut or color. Do a sample item as you repeat the instructions.

5. Provide a model for the student's response. Repeat the words or sentences as often as necessary.

6. Do not overload. Everything about English for the student is new and strange-sounding at first, and there are no "mental hooks" to hang new words on. Memory traces for new sounds disappear in a matter of seconds, especially if additional new sounds are immediately presented. Choose a pace that makes it easy for the student to succeed. Remember that students who feel smart learn faster.

7. Review. Each day, review the questions, answers and vocabulary from work already completed.

8. Be flexible. Use the student's reactions and needs to let you know how many pages to assign at a time, how often to review a page, or what additional material to add. Students may need to copy written work at times on separate paper.

9. Give feedback and reinforcement. When the student has finished a page, read it, comment on it, correct it and ask questions about it. Set standards for careful, neat work. Be honest in your praise and encouragement. Display the student's work in the classroom.

10. Test. Conduct an informal oral or reading test by asking the questions provided or having the student read the content. When the student has copied words or sentences, give a mini spelling test of appropriate grade level words. The tests will let you and the student know if more practice is needed.

11. Schedule time in your day for the ESL student. An abbreviated three-minute session may look like this:

a) teach the new words and read the sentences.

b) give instructions for completing the pages.

c) later, correct the pages and interact with the student.

If you have even less time, the following may occur:

a) one (or more) English-speaking classmate teaches the new lesson and gives instructions to the student.

b) the classmate corrects the pages and reteaches if necessary. You interact with the student when pages are complete, reinforcing and praising the student's accomplishment.

A thirty minute session with the student may look like this:

a) Review all the previous pages.

b) Give a mini spelling test by dictating one sentence or three words.

c) Check the test in the presence of the student; assign more copying work if it is needed.

d) Teach the brief oral lesson for the next page or pages. Practice with the student.

e) Give instructions for completing the pages. The student works at his or her seat.

f) Comment on the student's actions, using the present continuous or the past forms of the instructions you gave, i.e., "You are coloring the pictures. Now you are cutting the paper (drawing a line, writing the answer, etc.) Are you finished? You colored this very neatly. I like the pictures you drew. You wrote the word here. You need a capital letter here," and so on.

g) When the work is complete, give feedback. Comment on the coloring, check the answers, have the student read it and/or ask the student the question or questions that are on the page.

12) Keep track of progress. Use a "three star system." One star on the page indicates that the student understands and responds to the oral English on the page. Two stars means he or she can read the material. Three stars means he or she can spell it correctly.

13) Put the student's language to use in meaningful situations during the day. Greet him or her personally, give instructions in English, assign classroom jobs, comment on behavior and ask questions that have either yes or no answers or simple one-word answers.

14) Share the task of teaching with other available English speakers. Encourage the entire class to interact with the new student. Pair the student with an English-speaking buddy for room chores and errands that will involve contact with others. Train several interested English-speaking students in your class as teachers. This will multiply the instructional time available to the new student and draw him or her more rapidly into the social stream of the class. The enrichment benefits to the tutors is enormous as well, and this role should not be limited to your gifted students. Monitor their teaching to remind them to speak clearly and slowly and to repeat, praise and review. Your time with the ESL student can then be a final check after he or she has had lessons and practice with peers. Praise both the ESL student and "teachers" for their performances.

Teach peer tutors the terms objectives and procedures which occur in each set of directions. Be sure your tutors understand the concepts of modeling, demonstrating and repeating. If the tutor sits on the left of the student, he or she will be able to read the instructions printed down the left-hand side of the page.

15) Keep materials organized. Use a three hole punch on completed pages so the student can keep them in a three ring binder.

Name________________________________

On the street

Color the picture.

1. Objective: To learn the names of items in the street. Procedure: Point to the items in the picture and teach the words. Say, "What do you see in the picture?" Label any other things the student mentions. Say, "Copy the words (three) times each."

Name______________________________

2. Objective: To learn the words stop, crossing guard and the concept "cross at the corner." Procedure: Point to the street and say, "street." Point to the sidewalk and say, "Sidewalk. The two turtles are on the sidewalk. The turtles want to cross the street." Point to the corner and say, "Corner. They will cross the street at the corner." Point to the middle and say, "Should the turtles cross the street here? No, they should cross at the corner. What is this? (A car) A car is stopping. What does this say? (Stop) Who is this? He's a crossing guard. The crossing guard makes the car stop. Now the turtle children can cross the street. Color the picture."

3. Objectives: To learn the colors red, yellow, and green; to talk about safety and understand the traffic signals. Procedure: Say, "This is a traffic light. The top light says _____ (stop). What color means stop? Red. Find a red crayon." Point to the word "red" on the crayon to compare with the word "red" on the page. "The bottom light says ____ (go). What color means go? Green. Find a green crayon. What color is in the middle? Yellow. The middle light is yellow. Can you find a yellow crayon? Yellow means 'get ready to stop.' Color the top light red. Color the bottom light green. Color the middle light yellow." Ask questions about the lights and the meanings.

Name________________________________

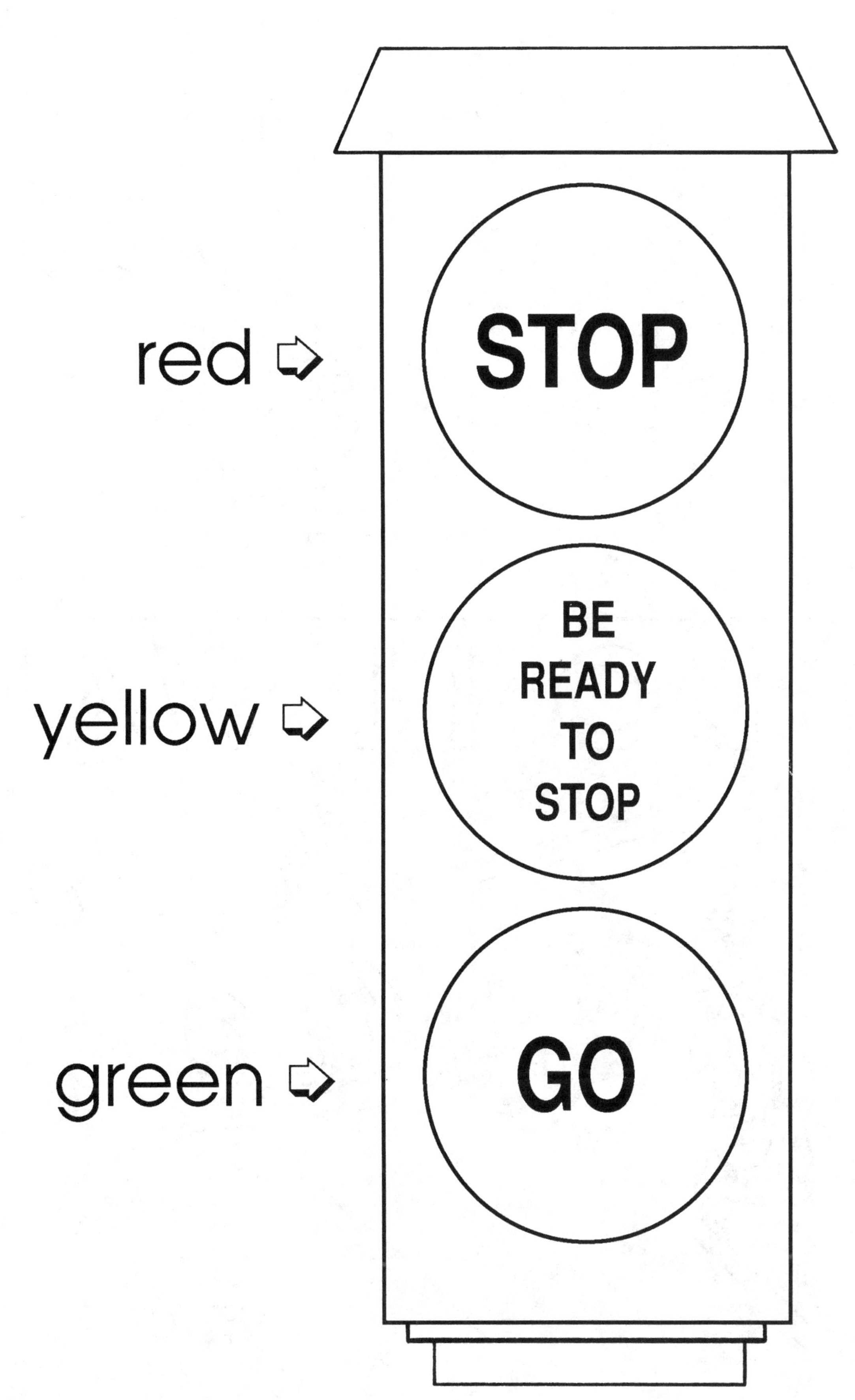

Color the lights.

Name________________________________

WALK

DON'T WALK

4. Objective: To read and understand traffic messages. Procedure: Point to the word "walk" and say, "Walk. The turtle is walking across the street." Point to the words "don't walk" and say, "Don't walk. The cars are going. The turtle is not walking. He is waiting. Color the letters 'W A L K' green. Color the letters in 'DON'T WALK' red. Color the picture."

Name________________________________

How do you come to school?

Check (✔) yes or no.

I walk to school. ☐ yes ☐ no

I ride a bicycle. ☐ yes ☐ no

I ride the bus. ☐ yes ☐ no

I ride in a car. ☐ yes ☐ no

5. Objectives: To understand and answer the question, "How do you come to school?"; to learn new words: walk, ride, bicycle, car, bus, check. Procedure: Read the question. Read each sentence, pointing to the picture. Say, "Check 'yes' or 'no.'" Demonstrate 'check.' When complete ask the student, "How do you come to school?" Help the student say the complete sentence. Say, "Color the pictures."

Name________________________________

What color is it ?

apple

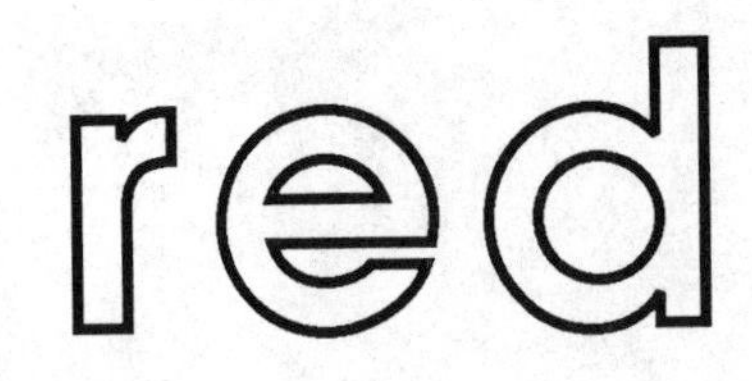

The apple is red.

tomato

The tomato is red.

cherries

The cherries are red.

roses

The roses are red.

6. Objectives: To understand and respond to the question "What color is it?"; to read sentences with singular or plural subjects and notice the use of the words is and are; to reinforce the color word red; to learn new words: apple, cherries, tomato, roses. Procedure: Point to the apple. Say, "Apple. This is an apple. What color is an apple? The apple is red." Point to the tomato. Say, "Tomato. This is a tomato. What color is it? The tomato is red." Continue. Say, "Read the sentences. Color the letters in the word 'red' red. Color the apple red. Color the tomato red. Color the cherries red. Color the roses red. Copy the sentences."

Name________________________________

What color is it ?

yellow

The sun is yellow.

sun

The bananas are yellow.

bananas

The turtle is green.

turtle

The plants are green.

plants

7. Objectives: To continue noticing the use of is and are; to reinforce the color words yellow and green; new words: sun, bananas, turtle, plants. Procedure: Point to the sun and say, "Sun. This is the sun. What color is the sun? Yellow. The sun is yellow. What else is yellow? Can you see anything yellow in this room? Look at the trees and plants. They are green. What else is green? Read the sentences. Color the word 'yellow' yellow. Color the turtle and the plants green. Color the word 'green' green. Copy the sentences."

Name________________________________

What color is it ?

blue

sky

The sky is blue.

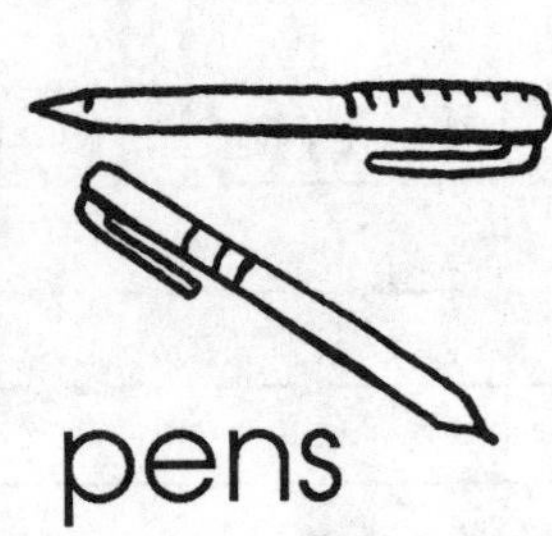

pens

The pens are blue.

white

shirt

The shirt is white.

clouds

The clouds are white.

8. Objectives: To learn the color names blue and white; to reinforce agreement between subject and verbs is or are; new words: sky, cloud, shirt. Procedure: Teach the words blue and white using crayons and chalk. Point out the window to the sky and say "sky." If it happens to be blue today, say, "The sky is blue." If not, point to the sky in the picture and say, "The sky is blue." Continue with each item on the page. Then say, "Color the pictures. Color the word 'blue' blue. Color the word 'white' white with chalk. Copy the sentences."

Name________________________________

What color is it ?

orange

orange

The orange is orange.

flowers

The flowers are orange.

purple

plum

The plum is purple.

grapes

The grapes are purple.

9. Objectives: To learn the colors orange and purple; to reinforce agreement between subject and verbs is or are; new vocabulary: orange, plum, flowers. Procedure: Use crayons to teach the color words orange and purple. Point to each item on the pages, and say the name of it for student to repeat. Then say, "Read the sentences." When complete, say, "Color the pictures. Copy the sentences."

Name______________________________

What color is it ?

black

crow

The crow is black.

cats

The cats are black.

brown

football

The football is brown.

chairs

The chairs are brown.

10. Objectives: To learn the colors black and brown; to reinforce agreement between subject and the verbs is and are; new words: football, cats, crow. Procedure: Teach the colors brown and black with crayons. Point to each item and say the name of it for student to repeat. Then say, "Read the sentences." When complete, say, "Color the pictures. Color the word 'brown' brown. Copy the sentences."

Name____________________________________

One	More than one
man	men
woman	women
child	children
foot	feet
tooth	teeth

11. Objectives: To learn irregular plural forms for common nouns; to reinforce vocabulary: man, woman, child, children, foot, tooth. Procedure: Point to the pictures as you say "One man, three men. Look. Is there an 's' here? No. One man, three men. There is an 'a' in man, (point) and 'e' in men. (Point.)" The student should repeat after you. Point to the woman and say, "One woman." Point to the women and say, "Two women." Continue for the rest of the page. Say, "Color the pictures. Copy the words."

Name________________________________

Add

$$\begin{array}{r} 2 \\ +\ 3 \\ \hline 5 \end{array}$$

Two
plus three
is five.

☆☆
☆☆☆
☆☆☆☆☆

$$\begin{array}{r} 6 \\ +\ 1 \\ \hline 7 \end{array}$$

$$\begin{array}{r} 9 \\ +\ 0 \\ \hline 9 \end{array}$$

12. Objectives: To learn to state problems in addition; to reinforce number words and their spelling: new words: add, plus. Procedure: Point to the title and say, "Add. Add two and three." Point to the numbers and the words for them as you read, "Two plus three is five. Now you read these problems." Then ask questions such as, "How much is two plus one? How much is five plus two? How much is three plus four?" Give several more problems stated in another way: "Add two and one. Add six and three. Add three and four. Add nine and zero. Now you ask me." After several questions that you answer, say, "Write the words for these problems."

Name________________________________

Add

$1 + 1 = 2$

One plus one (equals) two
(is)

$2 + 3 = 5$

$4 + 2 = $ ___

$6 + 1 = $ ___

---

13. Objective: To read an addition problem that is presented horizontally; new words: equals, problem. Procedure: Read the first number problem. "One plus one equals two." Point to the equals sign and say, "Equals." Read the problem again and say, "One plus one is two. 'Equals' and 'is' are the same. Now you read the next one." Continue until the student has read the problems. Say, "Write the words for these problems. Make other addition problems. Write the words for the problems."

Name ____________________________

Subtract

$$\begin{array}{r} 10 \\ -\ 4 \\ \hline 6 \end{array}$$

Ten ☆☆☆☆☆☆☆☆☆☆

minus four ☆☆☆☆

is six. ☆☆☆☆☆☆

$$\begin{array}{r} 9 \\ -\ 2 \\ \hline 7 \end{array}$$

$$\begin{array}{r} 8 \\ -\ 3 \\ \hline 5 \end{array}$$

14. Objectives: To learn to say a subtraction problem; to reinforce numbers. Procedure: Point to the title and say, "Subtract. Subtract four from ten." Point to the numbers and read, "Ten minus four is six." Say, "These are subtraction problems. Read the next problem." When complete, say, "How much is seven minus four? How much is six minus two?" Give a few more problems worded this way: "Subtract three from four. Subtract one from five," and so forth. Then say, "Now you ask me some subtraction problems." When complete, say, "Write the words for the subtraction problems here."

15. Objectives: To learn to read a horizontal subtraction problem; to reinforce number words. Procedure: Point to the numbers and read the words. Say, "Read these subtraction problems." When complete, say, "Write the words for these subtraction problems here. Make other subtraction problems. Write the words for them."

Name________________________________

Subtract

3 − 2 = 1

Three minus two (equals) one.
(is)

4 − 1 = 3

7 − 2 = 5

9 − 3 = 6

Name________________________

Count by tens

30 thirty

40 forty

50 fifty

60 sixty

70 seventy

80 eighty

90 ninety

100 one hundred

Count by fives.

Count by twos.

Copy the numbers.

16. Objectives: To learn to say, read and write the numbers thirty to one hundred; to learn to count by tens. Procedure: Point to the title and read it. Teach the numbers. Take care with the pronunciation of 'thirty,' 'fifty' and 'sixty' especially. Have student say the numbers up to forty. Then say, "Copy the numbers here." When complete, say, "Copy the numbers (three) times."

Name________________________________

Match the numbers

30	forty
50	thirty
40	sixty
60	fifty

80	eighty
100	seventy
70	ninety
90	one hundred

17. Objective: To reinforce reading of the numbers ten to eighty. Procedure: Point to the column of numbers and say, "Numbers." Point to the column of words and say, "Words. Draw a line from the number to the right word." Demonstrate if necessary.

Name________________________________

Money (coins)

penny = one cent (1¢)

heads tails = two cents (2¢)

nickel = five cents (5¢)

 =     

one nickel = five cents (5¢)

18. Objectives: To learn to recognize pennies and nickels and their values; new words: cents, heads, tails. Procedure: Using real pennies and nickels, teach the words penny and one cent, nickel and five cents. Teach the words and meanings of heads and tails. Gesture to show that you will toss a penny. Ask, "Heads or tails?" Student responds. Throw the penny. Depending on the result, say, "You win," or "You lose." Point to the title and say, "Money." Point out the cents sign and show how to make it. Say, "Copy the words for the cents here. Write the numbers for the cents here."

19. Objective: To learn to recognize dimes and quarters, and their values; to review pennies and nickels. New words: quarter, dime. Procedure: Place an assortment of pennies, nickels, dimes and quarters on the desk. Teach the names of the coins and their values. Put two nickels together. "How much is this? (ten cents): Two nickels equal one dime." Put two dimes and a nickel together. Say, "How much is this?" (twenty five cents): "Is this the same as a quarter?" Put different arrangements of the coins together for student to count the value. Then say, "Show me (thirty cents.)" Point to the words and ask student to read. Say, "Write the words for the cents here. Write the numbers for the cents here."

Name________________________________

Money (coins)

heads tails

= ten cents (10¢)

dime

= ten cents (10¢)

heads tails

= twenty five cents (25¢)

quarter

= twenty five cents (25¢)

heads tails

= fifty cents (50¢)

Name____________________

Money

half dollar = fifty cents (50¢)

heads tails = one hundred cents

(silver) dollar = one dollar ($1.00)

dollar bill ($1.00)

20. Objectives: To recognize a fifty-cent piece, a silver dollar, a dollar bill, and their values; to review other coins. Procedure: Use an assortment of coins to review the coins and values already learned. Teach the names and values for the new coins and the dollar bill. Place different combinations of coins together and ask, "How much is this?" Ask student: "Show me (fifty five) cents. Show me (one) dollar and (sixty five) cents." Have the student read the words as you point to each coin or bill. Say, "Copy the words here. This is how you write a dollar sign." (Demonstrate)

21. Objective: To reinforce recognition of the value of pennies, nickels, dimes and quarters. Procedure: Point to the coins in box # 1. Say, "How much is this? Write the answer here. Good, now do the next one."

Name________________________________

How much is this ?

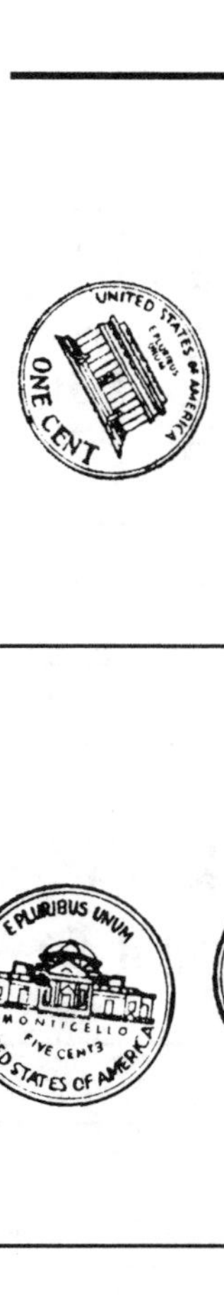

______ ¢

______ ¢

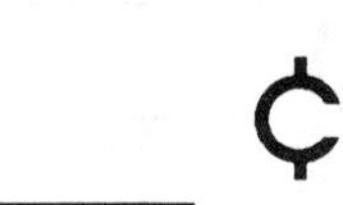

______ ¢

______ ¢

______ ¢

______ ¢

______ ¢

______ ¢

Name________________________________

Paper money

five dollar bill
$\$5^{\underline{oo}}$ or $5.00

ten dollar bill
$\$10^{\underline{oo}}$ or $10.00

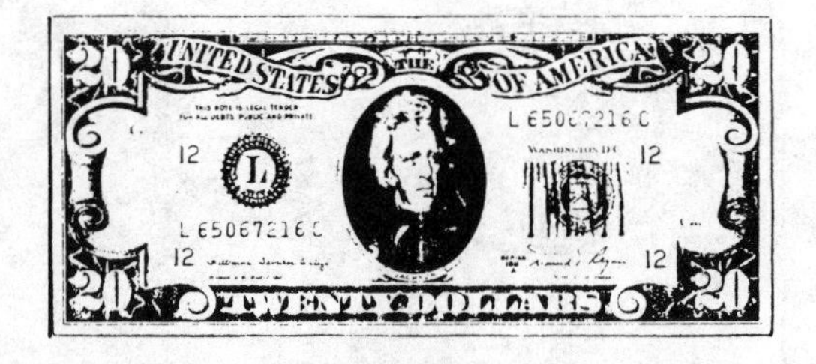

twenty dollar bill
$\$20^{\underline{oo}}$ or $20.00

$5.10 = five dollars and ten cents

$10.05 = ____________________

$6.20 = ____________________

22. Objective: To recognize paper money in different denominations. Procedure (optional): Show single, five, ten, and twenty dollar bills. Show that they are the same color and size. (Bills in other nations may be different colors and sizes; they are easier to distinguish than American bills.) Say, "Read the words. Copy the words here."

Name______________________________

Money

a. $2.50

b. $4.90

c. $20.00

d. $1.95 $3.75 $8.65

e. $7.45 $9.15 $22.01

f. $35.89 $42.98 $99.99

g. fourteen dollars and eight cents

h. twenty dollars and five cents

23. Objective: To read numbers expressed as dollars and cents; to write dollars and cents correctly. Procedure: If play money in ordinary denominations is available, use it to show quantities of money, and then write the quantities in dollars and cents. Say, "Read these money amounts. Write out the amount in words for a, b, and c. Practice reading the amounts in rows d, e, and f. Write the numbers for g and h."

24. Objectives: To understand and respond to the question, "How much is ___?"; to find out the costs of common student expenses; to write money amounts correctly.
Procedure: Point to the picture of the milk carton; ask, "How much is school milk? (15 cents) Write (15 cents) here." Repeat with each item. When the page is complete, say, "Make a sentence for each picture. School milk costs (is) (fifteen cents)." and so forth.

Name________________________________

How much is it ?

school milk

______

school lunch

______

telephone

______

bus

______

Name________________________________

Write words and sentences.

25. Objective: Review. Procedure: Select words and sentences from previous pages to dictate to student. Assist if necessary with spelling. May be used to test or reinforce spelling.

Name________________________________

Multiply

2 Two
x 3 times three
6 is six.

1
x 7
7

4
x 5
20

26. Objectives: To understand and respond to the question, "How much is (three) times (four)?"; to read and write multiplication problems. Procedure: Point to the title and say, "Multiply. These are multiplication problems. Multiply two times three. Two times three is six. Multiply one times seven. Multiply four times five. Multiply three times five. Now you give me some multiplication problems. Write the words for these multiplication problems."

27. Objective: To reinforce understanding of, saying and reading multiplication problems. Procedure: Point to the numbers and have the student read them. Say, "Write the sentences for these multiplication problems."

Name________________________________

Multiply

2 x 7 = 14

Two times seven equals fourteen.

3 x 4 = 12

5 x 2 = 10

6 x 1 = 6

Name________________________________

Divide

6 ÷ 2 = 3

Six divided by two equals three.

10 ÷ 5 = 2

12 ÷ 4 = 3

14 ÷ 2 = 7

28. Objectives: To understand and respond to the question "How much is (six) divided by (two)?"; to say and read division problems. Procedure: Point to the title and say, "Divide." Point to the first problem and say, "This is a division problem. Six divided by two equals three. Now you read it." Model it again if necessary. Say, "Read the other division problems. Now write the division problems here."

Name____________________________

Divide

$$\begin{array}{r} 2 \\ 4\overline{)8} \end{array}$$

Eight divided by four is two.

$$\begin{array}{r} 5 \\ 2\overline{)10} \end{array}$$

$$\begin{array}{r} 6 \\ 3\overline{)18} \end{array}$$

$$\begin{array}{r} 3 \\ 5\overline{)15} \end{array}$$

29. Objectives: To reinforce understanding and speaking about division problems; to learn the American form for writing division problems. (In some South American countries, the positions of the divisor and the quotient are reversed.) Procedure: Point to the dividend, then the divisor, then the quotient as you say, "(Eight) divided by (four) is (two)." Have student read the same problem. Say, "Read these division problems." When complete, say, "Write the words for the division problems."

Name________________________________

Write words and sentences.

30. Objective: Review. Procedure: Select words and sentences from previous pages to dictate to student. Assist if necessary with spelling. May be used to test or reinforce spelling.

Name________________________________

In my class

1.

Open your book.

2.

Write your name.

3.

Look at the blackboard.

4.

How much is 2 plus 2 ?

Answer the question.

31. Objectives: To understand and follow simple classroom instructions; to learn new words: open, look, answer. Procedure: Say, "Open your book." Demonstrate. "Open your (mouth, eyes, notebook, etc.) Close your (mouth, eyes, notebook)." Supply a sheet of paper and say, "Write (your name) (number five), (letters ABC). Look at the blackboard (window, map, your book). Answer this question: How much is one and one? Answer these questions: How much is school lunch? What's your name? Where are you from?" Say the four directions written on this page at random; have the student point to the correct picture, or say the number of the picture. Say, "Copy the sentences on another sheet of paper (three times)."

Name________________________________

Classroom rules

1.

Sit down.

2.

Listen.

3.

Raise your hand.

4.

Do your work.

32. Objective: To understand and follow rules in the classroom; new words: sit, raise, do. Procedure: Read the title. Point to each rule, read and demonstrate the meaning. Say the rules at random and have the student point to the correct picture. Say, "Read the rules. Copy the rules (three) times (on another sheet of paper)".

Name________________________________

In the gym

1.

Play a game.

2.

Run a race.

3.

Take turns.

4.

Keep score.

33. Objective: To understand and follow simple gym directions. Procedure: Read the title. Point to each picture, and read the sentence; have the student say it after you. Then say the sentences at random. Say, "What number is 'Keep score?'" (Number four.) Say, "Read the sentences. Copy the sentences on another sheet of paper (three) times."

Name________________________________

In music class

1.

Sing a song.

2.

Listen to music.

3.

Play the piano.

4.

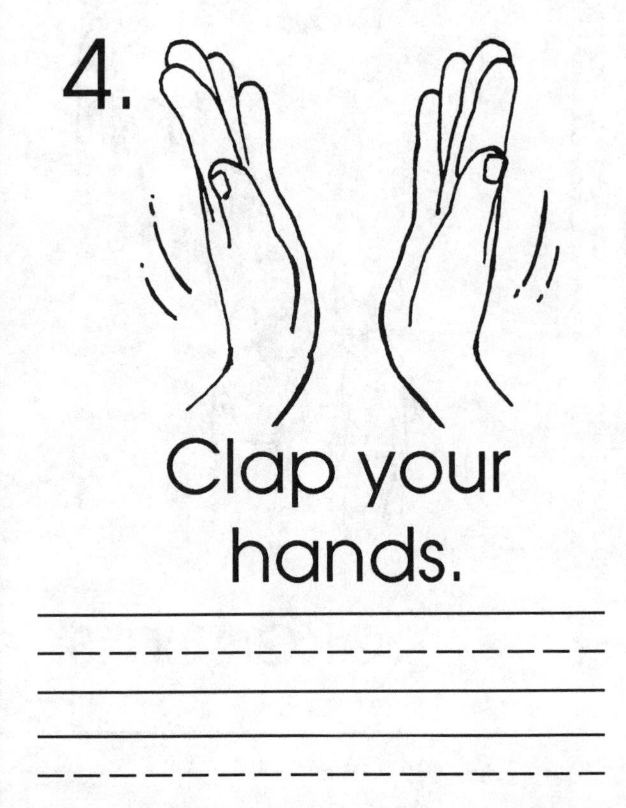

Clap your hands.

34. Objective: To understand and follow simple music class instructions. Procedure: Point to the title and read it. Point to each picture, read it and demonstrate if necessary. Have the student read after you. Say the sentences at random, and have the student point to the correct picture or tell you the number of the picture. Act out the directions and ask, "Which one am I doing?" (Optional: use the present continuous tense. "You are singing a song," and so forth.) Say, "Read the sentences." Copy the sentences on another sheet of paper (three) times."

35. Objective: To understand and follow simple art class instructions. Procedure: Point to the title and read it. Point to each picture and read the sentence as you demonstrate the action. Have the student read after you. Then say the sentences at random; have the student point to or tell you the number of the picture. Act out the directions and ask, "What am I doing? (I am drawing a picture.)" When complete, say, "Read the sentences. Copy the sentences on another sheet of paper (three) times."

Name______________________________

In art class

1.

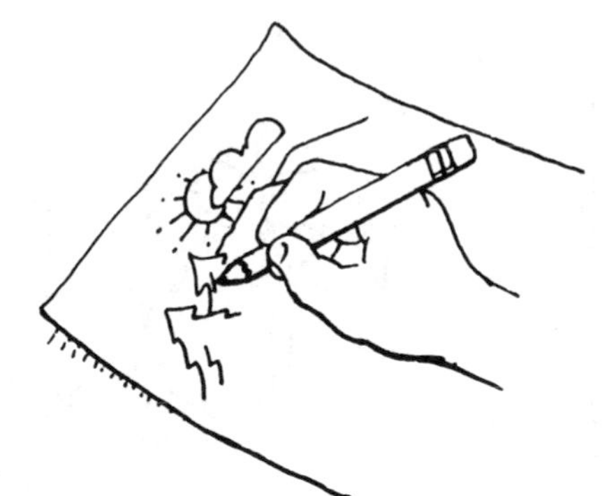

Draw a picture.

2.

Paint.

3.

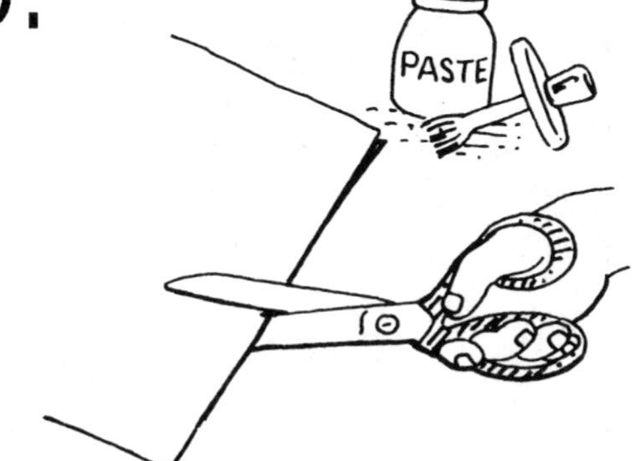

Cut and paste.

4.

Make something from clay.

Name________________________________

In the library

1.

Read a book.

2.

Listen to a story.

3.

Borrow a book.

4.

Return books.

36. Objective: To understand and follow simple library instructions. Procedure: Point to the title and read it. Point to each picture and read the sentence; have the student read it after you. Then say the sentences at random for the student to point to or tell you the number of the correct picture. Act out the directions and have the student guess what you are doing. When complete, say, "Read the sentences. Copy the sentences on another sheet of paper (three) times."

Name________________________________

In the hall

1\.

Line up.

2\.

Keep to the right.

3\.

Don't run.

4\.

Don't jump.

37. Objective: To understand and follow rules in the hall; new words: line up, keep to the right, don't run, don't jump. Procedure: Read the title. Point to each rule, read and demonstrate the meaning. Say the rule and have the student point to the correct picture or tell you the number of the picture. Say, "Read the rules. Copy the rules on another sheet of paper (three) times. Color the pictures."

Name________________________________

Lunch time

1.

Eat your lunch.

2.

Buy your lunch.

3.

Enjoy your lunch.

4.

Clean up.

38. Objectives: To understand and respond to instructions about lunch time. Demonstrate the meanings of the sentences as you read them. Say the sentences at random and have the student tell you the correct number. Ask, "Do you bring your lunch to school, or do you buy your lunch? What do you have for lunch today? Where do you throw the garbage? (In the trash can.)" Say, "Read the sentences. Copy the sentences on another sheet of paper (three times). Color the pictures."

Name____________________________

Match and write.

name book picture
song game

1. Open your ____________________.

2. Write your ____________________.

3. Sing a ____________________.

4. Play a ____________________.

5. Draw a ____________________.

39. Objective: To reinforce understanding, reading and writing of classroom directions. Procedure: Point to the words and say, "Read these words." Point to the first sentence and say, "Read this sentence. Which word will make a good sentence? (Book.) Write the word 'book' here. Now do the rest of the sentences."

Name________________________________

Color the clown.

1. She has blue eyes.
2. She has a red nose.
3. She has orange hair.
4. She has a green mouth.

40. Objectives: To become familiar with the sentence pattern "He/she has a (red) (nose)," to review and reinforce colors and parts of the face. Procedure: Say, "Who is this?" (She's a clown.) "Read sentence number one." Student reads. Say, "Now color the clown's eyes blue. Read the other sentences and color the picture the way the sentences tell you. Draw a picture of another clown. Write sentences to tell someone how to color the clown's face."

41. Objectives: To reinforce the sentence pattern, "He/she has a (brown) (hat);" learn clothing words: hat, tie, suit, shoes. Procedure: Point to the title and read it. Say each item of clothing and have the student repeat after you. Say the words at random for the student to point to the correct item. Then point to the words and have the student read them. Say, "Read the sentences. Color the picture."

Name________________________________

This is Mr. Brown.

1. He has a brown hat.
2. He has a brown tie.
3. He has a brown suit.
4. He has brown shoes.
5. He has a brown dog.

Name________________________________

This is Jim.

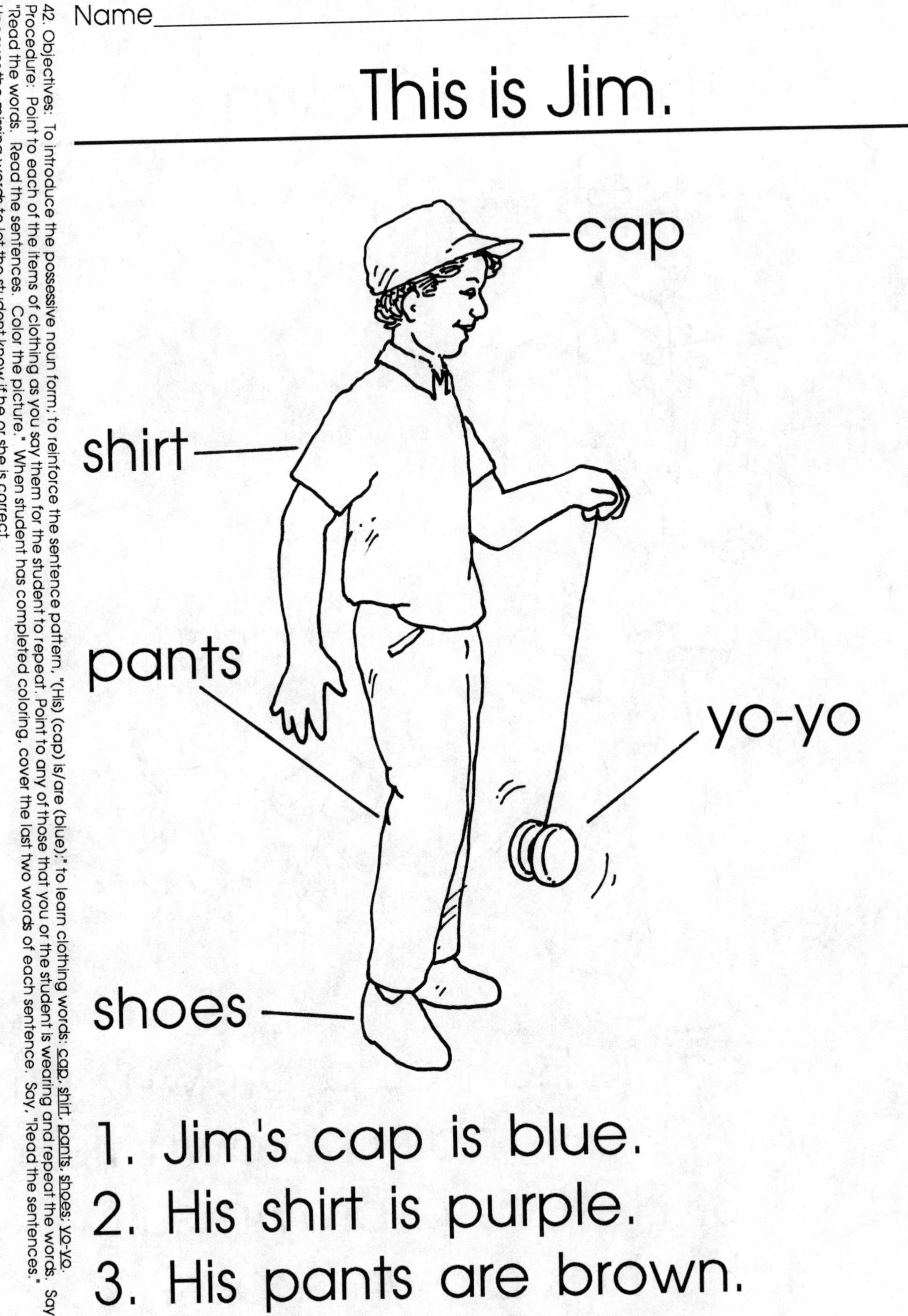

1. Jim's cap is blue.
2. His shirt is purple.
3. His pants are brown.
4. His shoes are black.

42. Objectives: To introduce the possessive noun form; to reinforce the sentence pattern, "(His) (cap) is/are (blue)."; to learn clothing words: cap, shirt, pants, shoes; yo-yo.
Procedure: Point to each of the items of clothing as you say them for the student to repeat. Point to any of those that you or the student is wearing and repeat the words. Say, "Read the words. Read the sentences. Color the picture." When student has completed coloring, cover the last two words of each sentence. Say, "Read the sentences." Uncover the missing words to let the student know if he or she is correct.

43. Objectives: To introduce possessive adjective her; to learn clothing words: socks, skirt, belt, blouse, ribbon. Procedure: Point to the items of clothing in the picture and say the words for the student to repeat. Say the words at random for the student to point to them. Point to items of clothing that you or the student are wearing for the student to name. Say, "Read the words. Read the sentences. Color the picture." When the student is finished, cover the first two words of each sentence. Say, "Read the sentences." Uncover the missing words so the student will know after each sentence if she or he is correct.

Name________________________________

This is Suzie.

1. Susie's blouse is yellow.
2. Her skirt is green.
3. Her socks are white.
4. Her shoes are red.

Name________________________________

Who is this ?

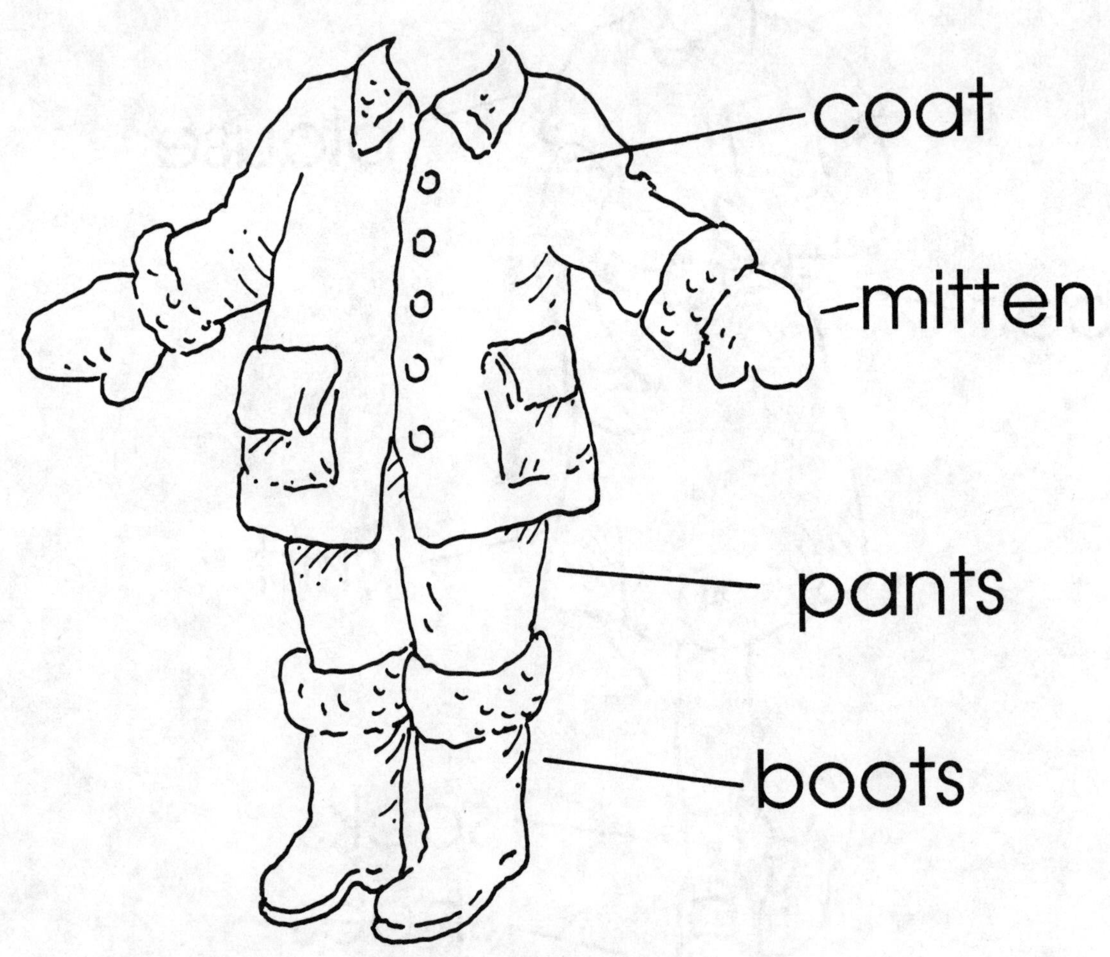

1. Draw the face.
2. Color the hat yellow.
3. Color the coat red.
4. Color the mittens orange.
5. Color the pants blue.

44. Objectives: To understand, read and respond to the directions, "Color the (boots) (black); draw (the face);" new clothing words: coat, mitten, boots. Procedure: Teach the names of the items of clothing. Then say, "Read the sentences. Color the picture the way the sentence tells you."

Name ______________________________

1. This is ______________________.

2. ____ 's __________ is brown.

3. Her / His _________ is red.

4. ____ ___________ are orange.

5. ____ _________ are blue.

6. ____ __________ are ______.

45. Objective: To reinforce the sentence pattern "(His/her) (coat) is/are (green)." to reinforce clothing plus color words. Procedure: Say, "Look at the person (on page 44). Who is this? This is ___. Write the name here. Is this a boy or a girl? Will you write 'his' or 'her'? What is yellow? Write the word here. Read the sentences. Do the rest of the page."

Name_______________________________

Match

1. cap ___

2. coat ___

3. mittens ___

4. boots ___

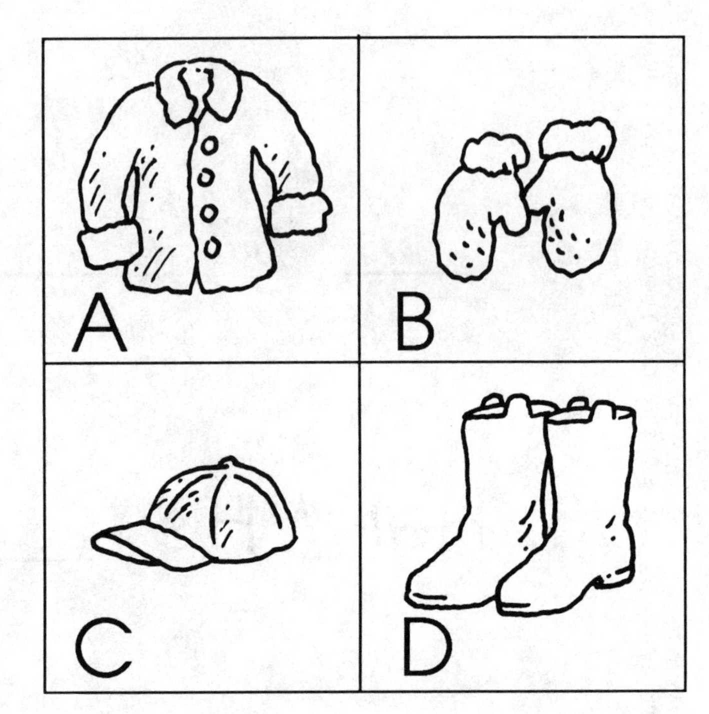

5. dress ___

6. shoes ___

7. socks ___

8. shirt ___

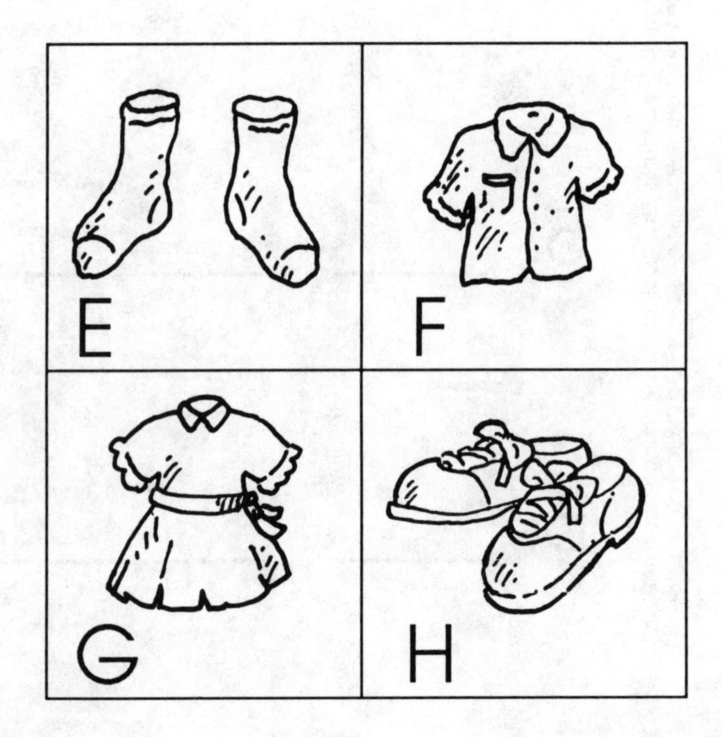

46. Objective: To reinforce reading of clothing words. Procedure: Read the title. Point to each of the items in the square for the student to name. Say, "Read number one. Where is the cap? (Student points.) A, B, C, D. What letter is cap? Cap is letter 'C'. Write the letter 'C' next to the word cap. Read the next word. Find the coat. Write the letter of the picture of a coat next to the word coat. Do the rest of the page."

Name________________________________

Draw

1. two red socks	2. four orange hats
3. six yellow ties	4. five black yo-yo's
5. one green chair	6. seven blue pencils

47. Objectives: To reinforce reading numbers, colors and clothing words; to understand and respond to directions, "Draw (number) (color) (noun)." Procedure: Point to the title and read it. Point to box number one and say, "Read the words. Now draw two red socks." Check as the student does this. Say, "Read the words in the other boxes. Draw all the pictures." When complete, check for color, number and item.

The calendar 19 __ __

SUNDAY	MONDAY	TUESDAY	WEDNESDAY	THURSDAY	FRIDAY	SATURDAY

48. Objectives: To introduce the calendar and the days of the week; to reinforce numbers up to 31. Procedure: Use the classroom calendar or another calendar for the current month. Point to it and say, "What's this? It's a calendar. What month is it? It's (October)." Point to the days of the week. Say, "These are the days of the week." Say the days for student to repeat after you. "What day is today?" (Tuesday) Point to today's date. Model the correct form of saying the date: "Today is (Tuesday), (October) (10) (1995)." Turn to the blank calendar. Say, "Copy the month here. Write the year here. What day of the week is (October) one? Write '1' here. Finish the calendar."

Name________________________________

The days of the week

Copy:

Sunday

Monday

Tuesday

Wednesday

Thursday

Friday

Saturday

49. Objective: To reinforce the names of the days of the week. Procedure: Review the days of the week. Help the student until he or she can say them in order. Then point to each word and say, "Read the days of the week. Copy each day two times."

Name________________________________

The days of the week

1. Sun. = ______________________

2. Mon. = ______________________

3. Tues. = ______________________

4. Wed. = ______________________

5. Thurs. = ______________________

6. Fri. = ______________________

7. Sat. = ______________________

50. Objective: To reinforce the days of the week; to learn the abbreviated forms for them. Procedure: Point to the abbreviation 'Sun'. Say, "Sunday. This is the short way to write 'Sunday.'" Gesture the meaning of the word 'short' with your hands. "What is the long way to write Sunday?" Gesture 'long' with your hands. "S U N D A Y. Write the long way to write the days of the week here."

Name____________________________

1. It's cloudy.
2. It's raining.
3. The girl has an ____________ .

51. Objectives: To learn words for rainy weather; to introduce the sentence pattern "It's (weather expression);" to reinforce alphabetical order. Procedure: Read the sentences to the student. Say, "Read the sentences. 'It's' is the same as 'it is'." Teach the words cloud, rain and puddle. Say, "What does the girl have? I don't know. Draw a line from A to B to C." When complete, say, "What is it? (an umbrella) "Read this sentence. Write the word 'umbrella' here. U M B R E L L A. Color the picture."

52. Objectives: To learn words for snowy weather, plus buttons, scarf, shovel; to reinforce the sentence pattern "It's (weather expression)." Procedure: Point to the snowman. Say, "What's this? It's a snowman. This is a snowman. The snowman has a hat. He has a scarf. Here are his buttons. How many buttons does he have? He has a shovel. The shovel is in front of the snowman. It's snowing. Read the sentences. Draw a snowwoman next to the snowman. Color the picture." When complete have student talk about the snowwoman he or she has drawn.

Name______________________________

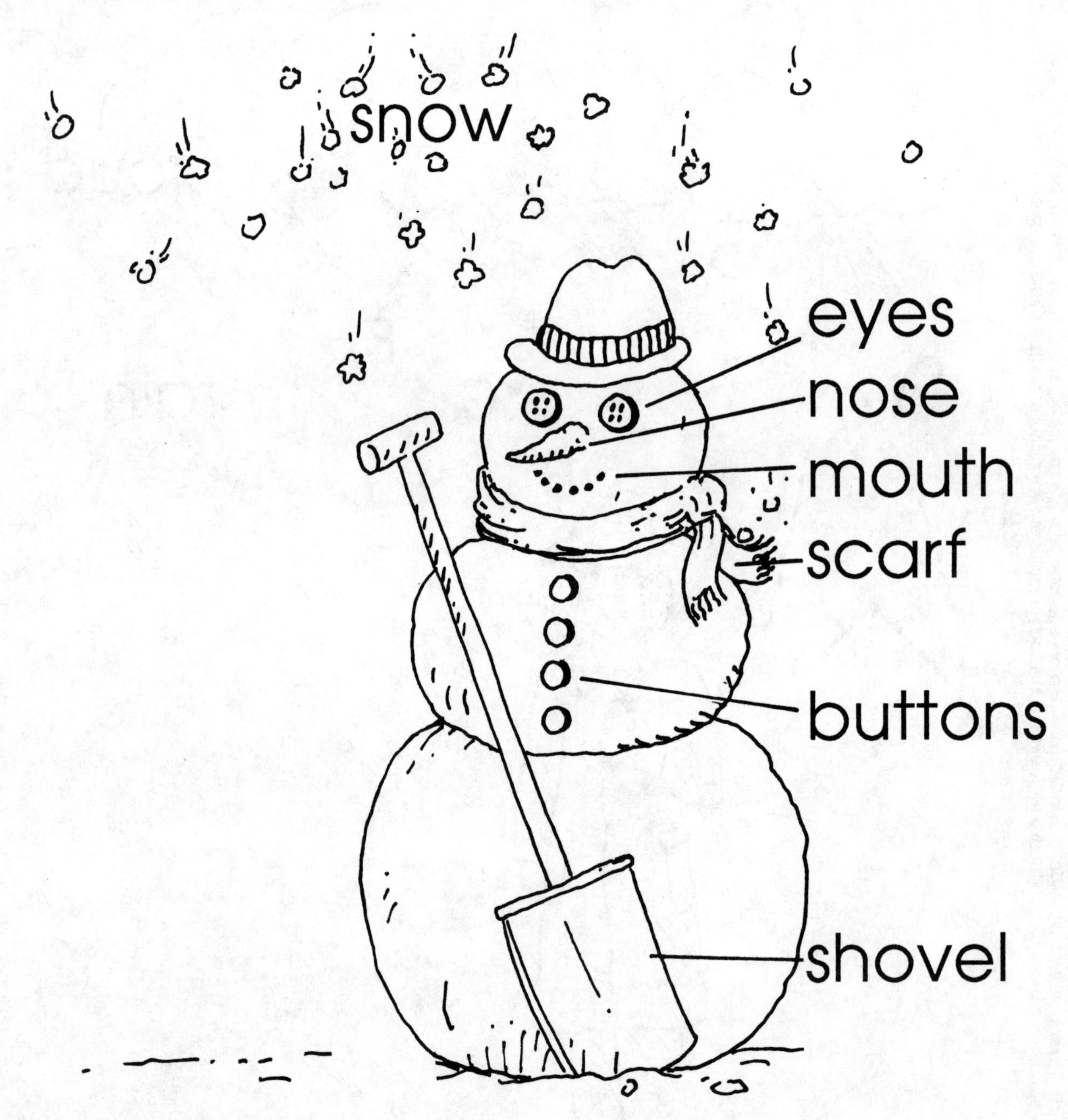

1. It's cold.
2. It's snowing.
3. I see a snowman.

4. Draw a snowwoman.

Name________________________________

1. It's hot.
2. It's sunny.

3. I see a ______________________ .

53. Objectives: To talk about hot weather; to reinforce sentence pattern "It's (weather expression)." Procedure: Say, "The sun is hot. It's hot. The dog is hot. He's lying in the shade. It's not raining. It's not snowing. Read the sentences. What do you see in the picture? Write the word here. Color the picture."

Name________________________________

What time is it ?

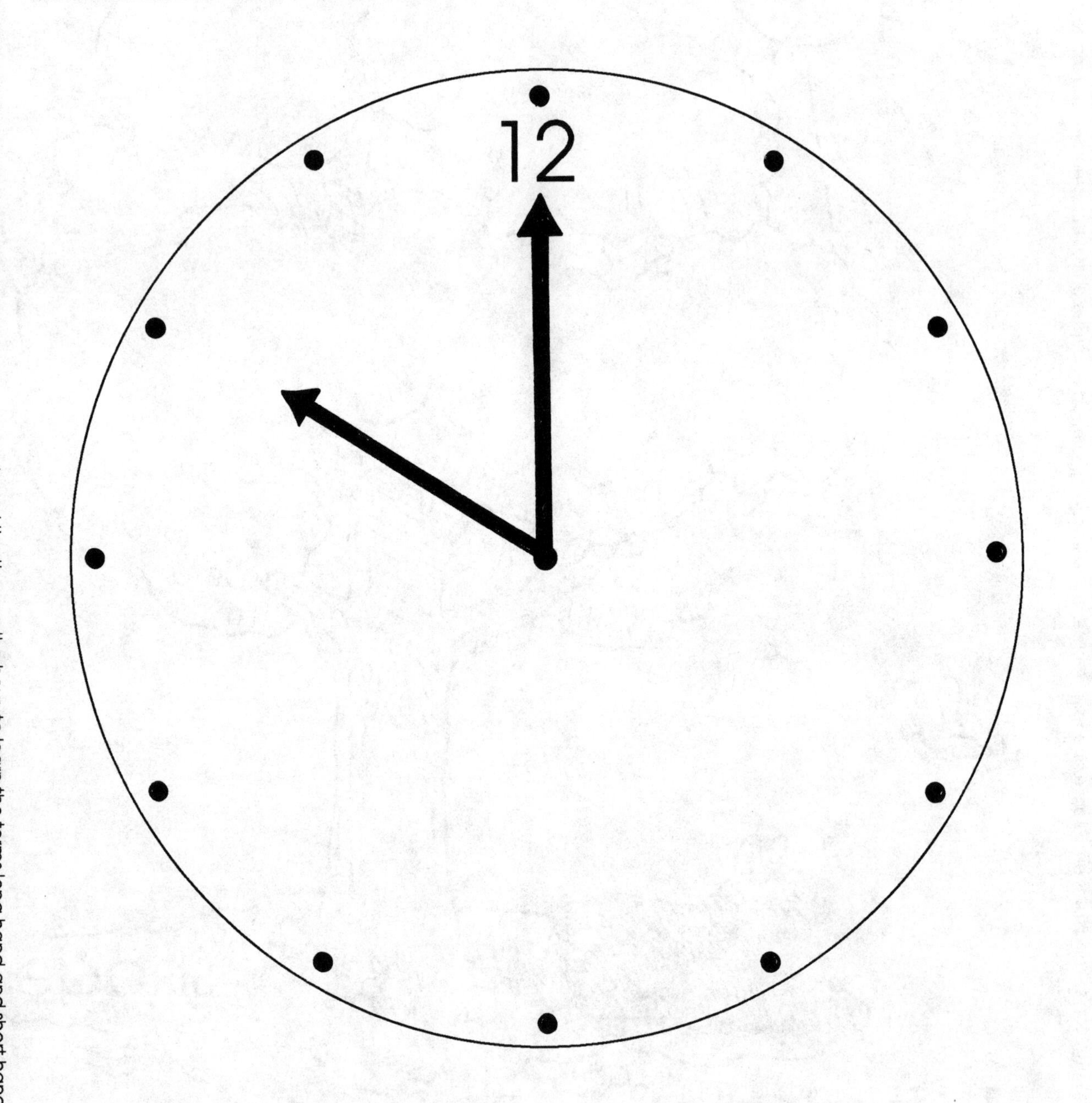

1. Write numbers on the clock.

2. It is ____________ o'clock.

54. Objectives: To understand the question, "What time is it?"; to say and read the time on the hour; to learn the terms <u>long hand</u> and <u>short hand</u>. Procedure: Point to the clock and say, "This is a clock." Point to the title and read it. Read the sentences. Say, "Write the numbers on the clock." When finished, say, "The clock has two hands." Teach the terms "long hand" and "short hand." Point to the long hand, then the short hand. Say, "The long hand is on the twelve. The short hand is on the ten. What time is it? Write '10' here. It is ten o'clock. It's ten o'clock." Write the contraction 'it's' under 'it is.'

55. Objectives: To reinforce telling time on the hour; to reinforce spelling of number words. Procedure: Say, "What time is it?" Point to each clock for the student to tell the time. Say, "Write 'It's six o'clock,' here. Write all of the times."

Name______________________________

What time is it ?

1. 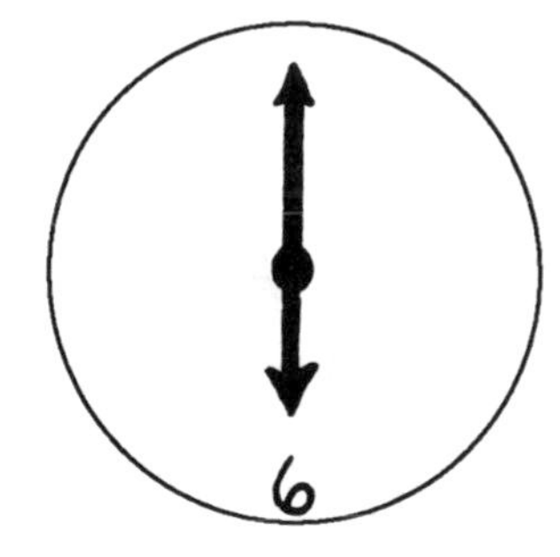

It's ______________________________

2. 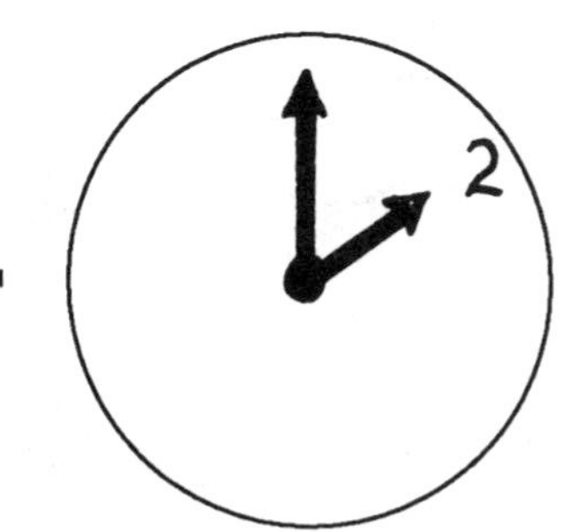

It's ______________________________

3. 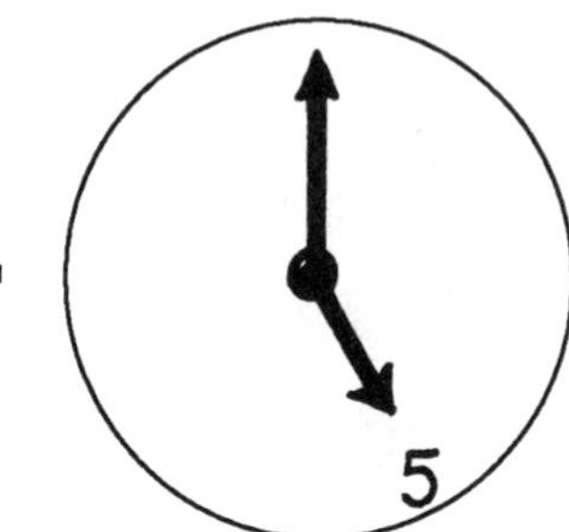

It's ______________________________

4. 

It's ______________________________

5. 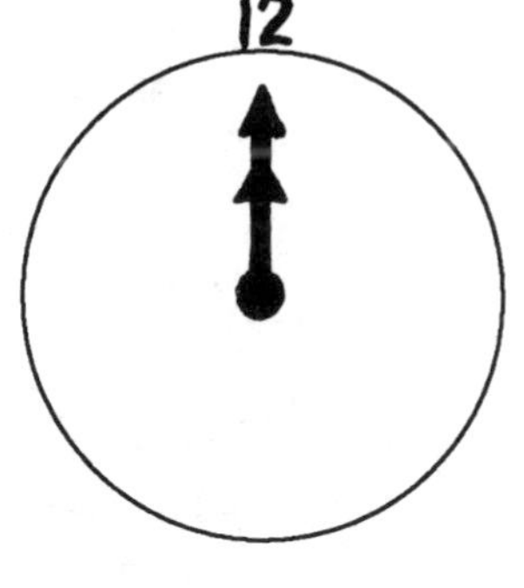

It's ______________________________

Name_______________________________________

1. School starts at

______________________ .

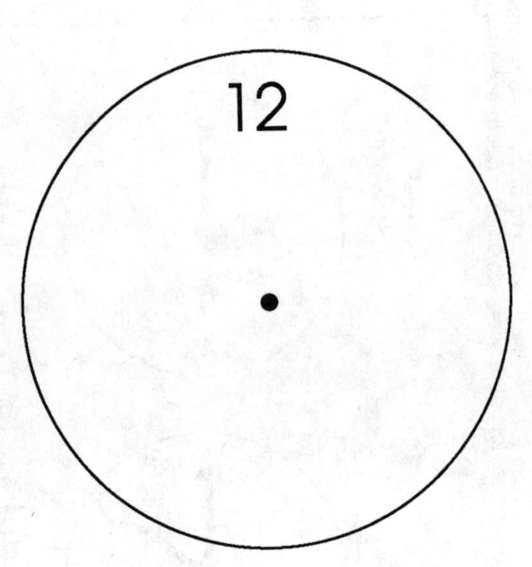

2. Lunch is at

______________________ .

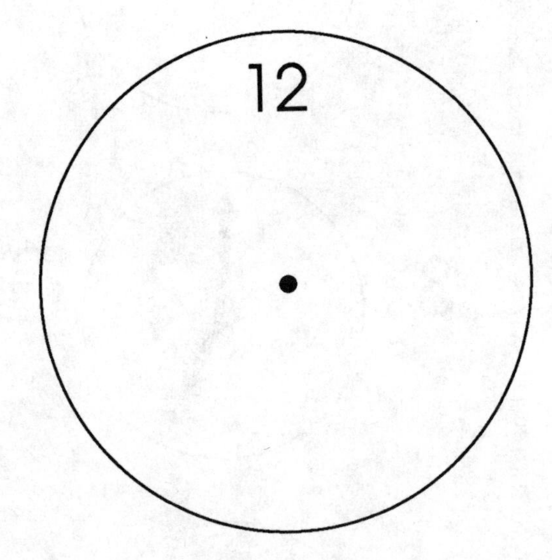

3. We go home at

______________________ .

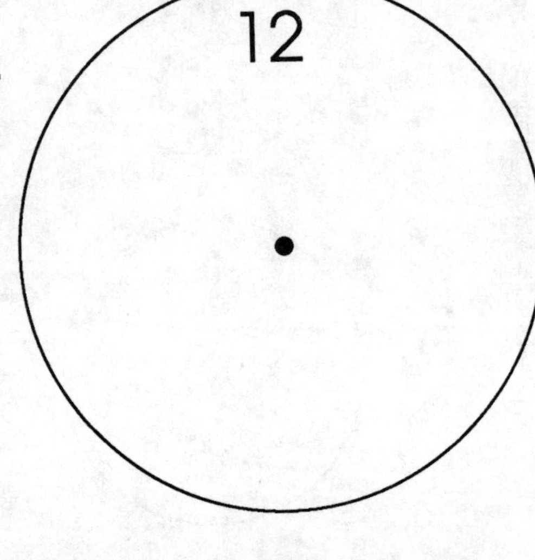

56. Objectives: To learn to say the time with the preposition at; to understand and respond to questions: "What time does school start? What time is lunch? What time do you go home?" Procedure: Write in the correct times that these events occur in your school. Read the sentence to the student. Teach how to say the time if it is not an exact hour, i.e. "Lunch is at twelve twenty." "We go home at three fifteen." Say, "Write the numbers on the clocks. Copy the sentences on a separate paper".

Name________________________________

The months of the year

1.

January

2.

February

3.

March

4.

April

57. Objectives: To learn the first four months of the year; to reinforce weather expressions. Procedure: Use a current calendar. Start with January and say each month of the year as you turn the page. Student may repeat after you. Then point to the picture # 1. Say, "January is the first month. It's cold in January. What do you see?" (A snowman.) Point to February. Say, "February is cold too. Valentine's Day is in February." Point to the heart. Point to pictures 3 and 4. "It's windy in March. It rains in April. Read the four months. Copy the names of the months. Color the pictures."

Name______________________________

The months of the year

5.

May

6.

June

7.

July

8.

August

58. Objectives: To learn the second four months of the year; to reinforce weather expressions; to learn action verbs for seasonal activities. Procedure: Review the first four months. Then say each month for student to repeat. Say, "There are flowers in May. Baby birds are born in June. It's hot in July. We can go to the beach. It's hot in August too. We can go on a picnic. Read the names of the months. Copy the names of the months. Color the pictures." When complete, ask questions that begin, "In what month . . .?"

59. Objectives: To learn the last four months of the year; to learn action words for activities in these months. Procedure: Review the first eight months. Point to each picture and say the month for the student to repeat. Point again; say, "School begins in September. Leaves fall off the trees in October. Thanksgiving is in November. It's cold in December. Christmas is in December." Ask questions that begin, "In what month . . .?" Say, "Copy the names of the months. Color the pictures."

Name______________________________

The months of the year

9.

September

10.

October

11.

November

12.

December

Name______________________________

The months of the year

1. There are ____ months in one year.

2. The first month is

______________________________.

3. This month is ____________________.

4. My birthday is ____________________ ______.

5. The last month is

______________________________.

60. Objectives: To reinforce the names of the months of the year; to learn first, last, this plus month; to understand and respond to the question, "When is your birthday?" Procedure: Point to the year on the calendar. Say, "What year is this? (1995)" Look at the previous three pages. Say, "How many months are in a year? (Count them.) What is the first month? The first month is January. What is the last month? When is your birthday? (Sing 'Happy Birthday' if the student doesn't understand the word birthday.) What month is this month?" Say, "Read the sentences. Write the answers. Copy the sentences on another sheet of paper."

61. Objective: Review. Procedure: Select words and sentences from previous pages to dictate to student. Assist if necessary with spelling. May be used to test or reinforce spelling.

Name_______________________

Write words and sentences.

Name________________________________

Let's be friends.

1.

2.

3.

4.

62. Objectives: To express friendship; to learn the language needed to invite others to play. Procedure: Read the title. Point to each word balloon and read it; have the student read after you. Indicate the meaning through facial expressions, smiling and pointing. Say, "Color the picture. Copy the sentences on another sheet of paper."

Name________________________________

On the ballfield

1.

Throw the ball.

2.

Catch the ball.

3.

Hit the ball.

4.

Strike (one).

63. Objective: To learn simple expressions used in playing ball. Procedure: Teach the words by demonstrating the action. Read the words as you point to the pictures. Say, "Read the words. Color the pictures. Copy the words (three times)."

64. Objective: To learn common action verbs on the playground. Procedure: Teach the words by demonstrating the action. Read the words as you point to the pictures. Say, "Read the words. Color the pictures. Copy the words (three times)."

Name______________________________

On the playground

1.

swing

2.

jump

3.

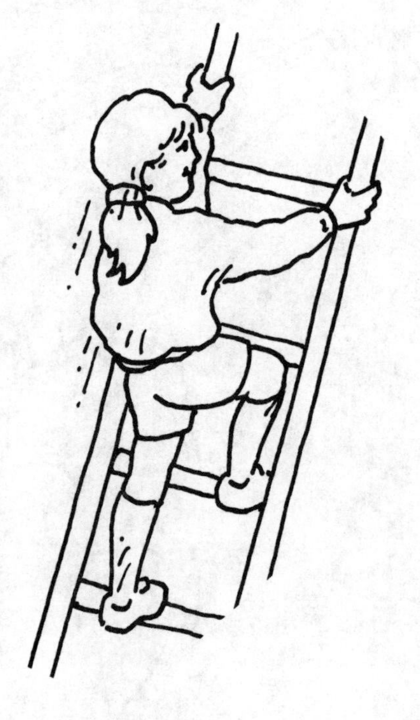

climb

4.

slide

Name________________________________

On the playground

1.

ball

2.

jump rope

3.

hopscotch

4.

tag

65. Objective: To learn common game playing expressions. Procedure: Point to picture # 1. Say, "This boy and girl are going to play baseball. This girl wants to play. She says, 'Can I play?' The boy says 'OK.'" For picture # 2, say, "The children are playing jump rope. The boy had his turn. He gives the jump rope to the girl. He says, 'It's your turn.'" For # 3 say, "The children are playing hopscotch. The boy stepped on a line. (Point.) He's out. The girl is saying, 'You're out.' Now it's my turn." For # 4 say, "The children are playing tag. This girl is 'it.' She tags (demonstrate) this boy. She says, 'You're it.' Now it's his turn to be 'it'. Now it's your turn to read. Copy the sentences on another sheet of paper. Color the pictures."

Name________________________________

The Happy-Sad-Mad Game

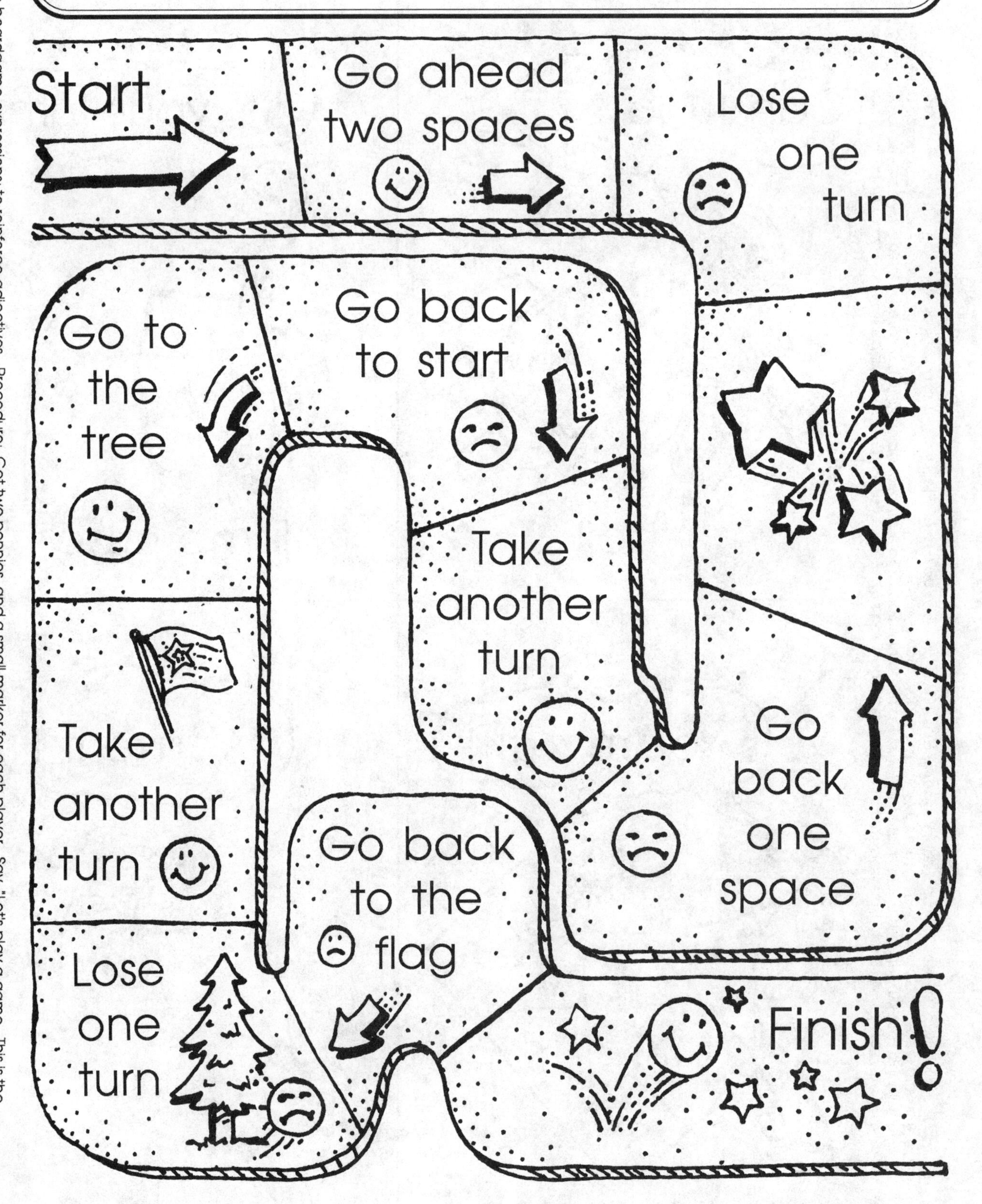

66. Objectives: To learn boardgame expressions; to reinforce adjectives. Procedure: Get two pennies, and a small marker for each player. Say, "Let's play a game. This is the Happy-Sad-Mad Game." Say, "Shake the pennies. Two heads means go two spaces. (Demonstrate). One head and one tail mean go one space. Two tails means go back one space. (Demonstrate). When you land on a space, you read the sentence. Do what it tells you. Then say, 'I am happy' or 'I am sad' or 'I am mad.' If you finish first you are the winner! Are you happy?"

Name____

1.

2.

3.

4.

67. Objectives: To learn sentence patterns "That is/those are (nice) (shirt/s)," new words: nice, pretty, funny, beautiful. Procedure: Compliment the student on some item of clothing or previous pages that have been colored, saying "That's a (nice) (shirt)." Read the sentences for the picture and have the student read after you. Say the sentences at random as student listens and tells you the number of the sentence that you are saying. Say, "Read the sentences. Copy the sentences on another sheet of paper. Color the pictures."

Name________________________________

1.

2.

3.

4.

68. Objectives: To learn the sentence patterns "This is/these are (good) (book/s)." new words: good, bad, right, wrong. Procedure: Read the sentences for each picture and have student read after you. Say the sentences at random and have student tell the number of the sentence. Student reads the sentences. Say, "Color the picture. Copy the sentences on a separate sheet of paper."

Name________________________________

Shapes

1.

circle

2.

square

3.

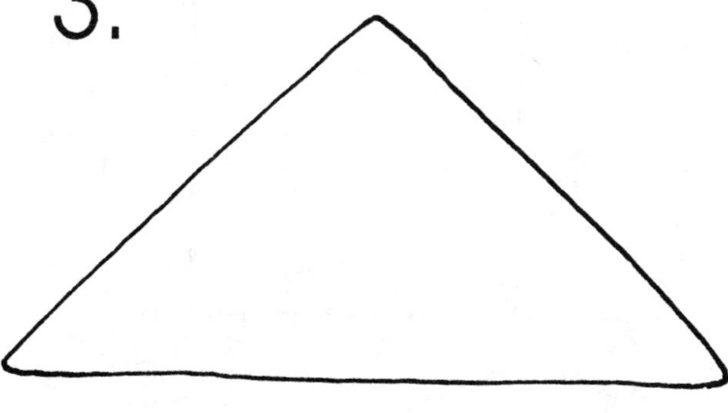

triangle

4.

rectangle

5.

star

6.

heart

69. Objective: To learn the names of shapes. Procedure: Prepare cut out circles, squares, triangles, rectangles, stars and hearts. Teach the words for these shapes. Say, "These are shapes." Read the title. Point to each picture as student reads or says the name of the shape. Say, "Color the shapes. Copy the words on a separate paper."

Name________________________________

1. Color the circles yellow.
2. Color the triangles green.
3. Color the squares blue.
4. Color the rectangles brown.

70. Objectives: To reinforce the names of shapes; to follow directions. Procedure: Say, "Look at the picture. How many circles can you see? (Three.) How many rectangles can you see? (Four.) How many triangles can you see? (Five.) How many squares can you see? (Five.) Read the sentences. Color the picture the way the sentences tell you."

Name____

Sizes

1.

a big circle

2.

a little circle

3.

a tall tree

4.

a short tree

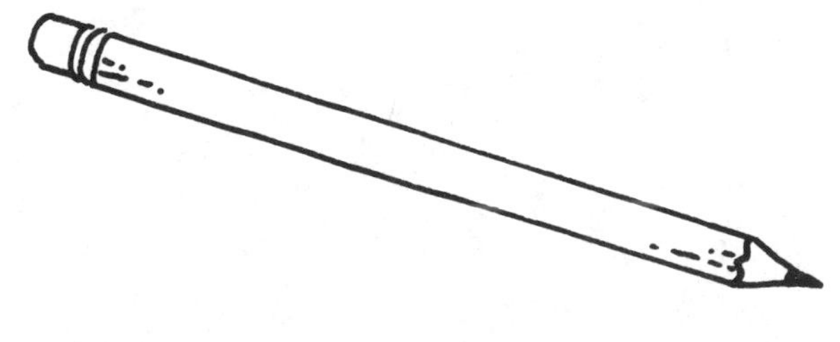

a long pencil

a short pencil

71. Objectives: To learn the adjectives big, little, tall, short, long; to reinforce adjective + noun word order. Procedure: Point to the top two pictures, saying "a big circle; a little circle." Point to and name other objects on your desk or in the class that are big or little. Point to pictures # 3 and 4, say "A tall tree, a short tree." Point to and describe pictures of tall and short buildings or people. Do the same with pictures 5 and 6. Say each phrase at random and have the student tell you the number of the correct picture. Say, "Read these phrases. Color the picture. Copy the words on a separate sheet of paper."

Name________________________________

Draw

Draw one big blue square.

Draw five little red stars.

Draw two long yellow buses.

Draw four tall orange hats.

72. Objective: To read and understand instructions, reinforcing sizes and colors. Procedure: Have student read the sentences. Say, "Draw a picture to show (one) (big) (blue) (square). Complete the page."

Name______________________________

in

1.

in the box

2.

in the house

3.

in the pocket

4.

in the bag

73. Objectives: To understand and use the preposition in; to respond to the question "Where is ____?" with a prepositional phrase answer; new words: box, pocket, bag.
Procedure: Point to the pictures as you give a complete sentence for each picture; the student reads the phrases after you. Ask, "Where is (the cat)? In (the box)." And so forth. Give instructions for the student to follow with some small objects on the desk: "Put the (penny) in the (box)." Point to each picture and say, "Make a sentence for each picture. (The cat is in the box.) (And so forth.) Color the pictures. Copy the words. Write complete sentences on a separate sheet of paper."

Name________________________________

on

1.

on the table

2.

on his head

3.

on the floor

4.

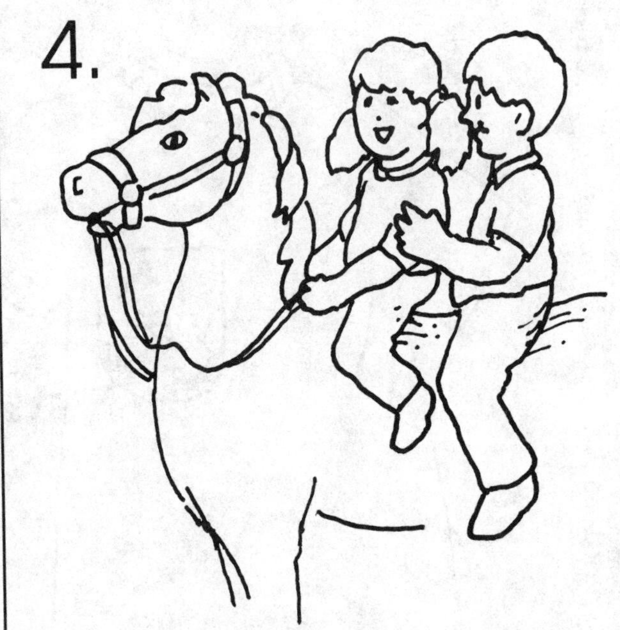

on the horse

74. Objectives: To understand and use the preposition on; to reinforce prepositional phrase word order; new words: floor, horse. Procedure: Read the title; point to each picture and say a complete sentence. Have the student read the prepositional phrase after you. Say each phrase at random and have the student tell you the number of the correct picture. Say, "Read the phrases under each picture." Give instructions for the student to follow with small objects on the desk: "Put the (pencil) on the (paper). Make a sentence for each picture. (The book is on the table.) Copy the words. Write complete sentences on another sheet of paper. Color the pictures."

75. Objectives: To understand and use the preposition next to; to reinforce prepositional phrase word order. Procedure: Gather small objects on the desk. Give the student instructions, and demonstrate: "Put the (crayons) next to the (pencil case)." Point around the room at children or objects and say, "(Dan) is next to (Jennifer)." Point to each picture and give a complete sentence. Have the student read the phrase. Say, "Make a sentence for each picture. Copy the words here. Color the pictures. Write the sentences on another sheet of paper."

Name________________________________

next to

1.

next to the blackboard

2.

next to the house

3.

next to the book

4.

next to the door

Name______________________________

On the farm

1. pig ___
2. horse ___
3. cow ___
4. sheep ___
5. goat ___
6. cat ___
7. dog ___
8. chickens ___
9. rooster ___
10. bee ___
11. mouse___
12. flies___

76. Objectives: To learn to say and read names of farm animals; to reinforce sentences with the prepositions in, on, next to. New words: farm, barn, plus animal words. Procedure: Read the title. Say, "This is a farm. Here is a barn. There are many animals on the farm." Teach the animal names. Point to the words and read, having the student read after you. Point to the first word and say, "What's this word?" (pig) "Where is the pig? What letter is next to the pig? (L) Write the letter 'L' next to the word pig. Do the rest of the words. Color the picture. Copy the names of the animals on a separate sheet of paper."

Name____________________________________

Where is it ?

1. The horse is ____.

2. The rooster is ____.

3. The goat is ____.

A. on the barn.

B. next to the barn.

C. in the barn.

77. Objective: To distinguish in, on, next to. Procedure: Say, "Look at the picture of the farm. Where is the horse? (in the barn) Where is the rooster? (on the barn) Where is the goat?" (next to the barn). Read the title and the first sentence fragment. Say, "Finish the sentence. The answer is here. (Point to the three answers.) Which is correct? The horse is on the barn, the horse is next to the barn, or the horse is in the barn? Write the complete sentences on a separate sheet of paper."

Name______________________________

over

78. Objectives: To understand and use the preposition over; to reinforce prepositional word order; new words: airplane, city, balloons, birds. Procedure: Hold an object over the desk and say, "The (pen) is over the desk." Point to each picture and make a sentence for it. "The airplane is over the city." (And so forth.) Say the sentences at random and have the student tell the number of the picture. Say, "Read the phrases." Make a complete sentence for each picture. Color the picture. Copy the words here. Write complete sentences for each picture on a separate sheet of paper.

1.

over the city

2.

over the table

3.

over the trees

4.

over the house

79. Objective: To understand and use the preposition under; to reinforce prepositional word order. Procedure: Place several objects under other objects on and around the student's desk. Make sentences. "The (dictionary) is under the (desk)." Then give directions to follow: "Put the (pen) under the (book)." Read the title and the phrases under each picture and have the student read after you. Say a sentence for each picture and have the student tell you the number of the picture. Say, "Copy the words. Color the pictures. Write a complete sentence for each picture on a separate sheet of paper."

Name ______________________

under

1.

under the car

____

2.

under the umbrella

____

3.

under the tree

____

4.

under the chair

____

80. Objectives: To understand and use the preposition behind; to reinforce prepositional word order. Procedure: Line up several toy objects on the desk. Point to each as you say, "(The horse) is behind the (truck)." Point to students in the room and say "(Dan) sits behind (Jane)." Give directions to follow, such as "Put the (cat) behind the (horse). Go behind (another student)." Read the title and the phrases under each picture. Make sentences about the pictures at random and have the student tell which picture it is. Say, "Read the phrases. Make a complete sentence for each picture. Copy the words here. Color the pictures. Write complete sentences on another sheet of paper."

Name____

behind

1.

behind Jim

____

2.

behind the door

____

3.

behind the women

____

4.

behind the trees

____

Name________________________________

Draw

1. The bird is over the house.

2. The mouse is under the hat.

3. The car is behind the bus.

81. Objective: To read and understand sentences with prepositions. Procedure: Have student read sentences. Model each one if necessary.Say, "Draw a picture to show the (bird) is (over) the (house)."

Name________________________________

In the woods

1. deer ___
2. bird ___
3. squirrel ___
4. rabbit ___
5. fox ___
6. skunk ___
7. raccoon ___
8. bear ___
9. owl ___

82. Objective: To learn the names of animals that live in the woods. Procedure: Teach the names of the animals. Read the words and have the student read after you. Point to the first word. "What's this? (Deer) Where is the deer? What letter is next to the deer? (I) Write the letter "I" next to the word deer. Do the rest of the animals. Color the picture. Copy the names of the animals on a separate sheet of paper."

Name________________________________

Where are the animals ?

1. The deer is __________ the ______ .

2. ______________________________

3. ______________________________

4. ______________________________

5. ______________________________

6. ______________________________

83. Objectives: To review and reinforce prepositions; to reinforce the names of animals. Procedure: Look at the picture on page 82 and ask, "What animal is behind a tree? (A deer) What animal is behind the rabbit? (A fox) What animal is in a tree? (An owl) What animal is on a nest? (A bird) What animal is under a squirrel? (A skunk) What animal is over the rabbit? (A bird)" Say, "Make a sentence telling where the (deer) is. Write sentences that tell where the animals are."

Name________________________________

In the jungle

1. monkey ___
2. zebra ___
3. lion ___
4. giraffe ___
5. hippo ___
6. elephant ___
7. alligator ___
8. bird ___

84. Objective: To learn the names of wild animals. Procedure: Teach the names of the animals in the picture. Read the animal words, and have the student read after you. Point to the first word. "What's this word? (Monkey) Where is the monkey? What letter is next to the monkey? (F) Write the letter 'F' next to the word monkey. Do the rest of the animals. Color the picture. Copy the names of the animals on a separate sheet of paper."

Name______________________________

Where are the animals ?

1. The hippo is ______ the water.

2. ______________________________

3. ______________________________

4. ______________________________

5. ______________________________

6. ______________________________

85. Objectives: To write sentences using prepositional phrases; to reinforce spelling of animal words. Say, "Write sentences that tell where the animals are." Refer to page 84.

86. Objective: To learn the names of animals that live near or in the water. Procedure: Teach the names of the animals in the picture. Read the words as student reads them after you. Point to the first word. Say, "What's this word? (Frog) Where is the frog? What letter is next to the frog? (D) Write the letter 'D' next to the word 'frog.' Do the rest of the animals. Color the picture. Copy the names of animals on a separate sheet of paper."

Name_________________________________

Near the water

1. frog ___
2. fish ___
3. duck ___
4. turtle ___
5. insect ___
6. snake ___
7. bird ___

Name________________________________

Where are the animals ?

1. ______________________________

2. ______________________________

3. ______________________________

4. ______________________________

5. ______________________________

6. ______________________________

87. Objectives: To write sentences using prepositional phrases; to reinforce names of animals. Procedure: Ask, "What animal is next to a tree? What animal is in the water? What animal is over the grass? What animal is on a rock? What animal is behind a little fish? Write sentences about the animals that tell where they are."

88. Objective: To learn the names of animals that live in and near the ocean. Procedure: Teach the names of the animals. Read the words and have the student read after you. Read the first word. Say, "What's this word? (Fish) Find a fish. What letter is next to the fish? (H) Write the letter 'H' next to the fish. Do the rest of the animals. Copy the names of the animals. Color the picture."

Name________________________________

By the sea

1. fish ___
2. person ___
3. whale ___
4. shark ___
5. crab ___
6. clam ___
7. starfish ___
8. dolphin ___
9. octopus ___

Name________________________________

Where are the animals ?

1. ________________________________

2. ________________________________

3. ________________________________

4. ________________________________

5. ________________________________

6. ________________________________

89. Objectives: To write sentences using prepositional phrases; to reinforce spelling of the names of animals. Procedure: Look at page 88. Ask, "What animal is behind a little fish? (Shark) What animal is next to a person? What animals are in the water? What animals are on the land? Write sentences that tell where the animals are."

Name________________________________

Are you . . .

1.

very big ?

☐ Yes, I am.

☐ No, I'm not.

2.

strong ?

☐ Yes, I am.

☐ No, I'm not.

3.

funny ?

____

- - - - - - - - - - - - - - - - - - -

____

4.

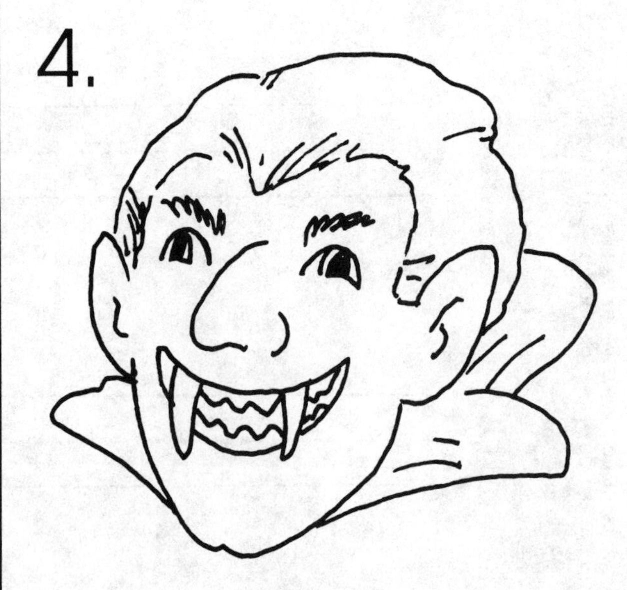

dangerous ?

____

- - - - - - - - - - - - - - - - - - -

____

90. Objectives: To understand and respond to the question pattern, "Are you (adjective)? Yes, I am; no, I'm not;" new words: very, strong, funny, dangerous. Procedure: Point to the first question and ask, "Are you very big?" Read the two answers. Say, "Make a check in the box next to your answer. Look at picture number two. 'Are you strong?'" The student checks the box and reads his or her answer. Continue, demonstrating the meanings of the words if necessary. The student writes the answers for # 3 and 4. Say, "Read the questions and answers again. Copy the complete questions and answers on another sheet of paper. Color the pictures."

Name________________________________

Write sentences.

91. Objective: To practice writing complete sentences describing self. Procedure: Point to the pictures. Say, "Are you (strong)?" When student answers, model a complete sentence. Have student repeat it. Do all four pictures orally. Have student write complete sentences on the page.

Name________________________________

are

are not

(very)

big

dangerous

strong

funny

beautiful

92. Objectives: To understand, use and read affirmative and negative sentence patterns: (Horses) are (not) (beautiful); to use the word "and" to join words; to reinforce animal and adjective vocabulary. Procedure: Point to the first word (horses) then to "are," and then to "big." Say, "Horses are big. Can you make other sentences about horses? Can you make a sentence about horses with two of these words? (Horses are big and strong.) Can you make a sentence about horses that has the word "not" in it? (Horses are not funny.) Can you make a sentence about two animals? (Horses and elephants are strong.) How many sentences can you make?"

93. Objectives: To write the sentence pattern: (Nouns) are/are not (adjective); to reinforce the spelling of animal names and adjectives. Procedure: Say, "Look at page 92. Make five sentences. Write the complete sentences here."

Name________________________________

1. Horses are big and strong.

2. ______________________________

3. ______________________________

4. ______________________________

5. ______________________________

6. ______________________________

Name________________________________

Where do they live ?

A.	B.	C.
in a tree	in the woods	in the jungle
D.	**E.**	**F.**
in the water	in a house	on a farm

94. Objectives: To tell where animals live; to use the verb live and a prepositional phrase; to reinforce words for animal homes. Procedure: Read the title question. Review the words for the pictures. Point to the (bears) and ask, "Where do (bears) live?" Student points to (the woods). "Yes, (bears) live (in the woods). Can you say that? Continue with the other animals. Make a sentence for the rest of the animals. Color the pictures."

Name________________________________

95. Objective: To write complete sentences telling where animals live. Procedure: Read the first sentence and have the student read after you. Look at page 94. Say, "Write five sentences here that tell where the animals live."

1. Bears live in the woods.

2. ________________________________

3. ________________________________

4. ________________________________

5. ________________________________

6. ________________________________

96. Objective: To create questions and answers of the pattern: "What animals have (adjective) (noun)? (Rabbits) have (short) (tails)." Procedure: Read the title plus the first choice of words. "What animals have short tails? (Rabbits.) Rabbits have short tails. What animals have long tails? (Lions, horses, alligators and snakes) have long tails." Have student ask the question and you answer. Then you ask the questions and student answers.

Name________________________________

What animals have . . .

short		long
	1. tails ?	 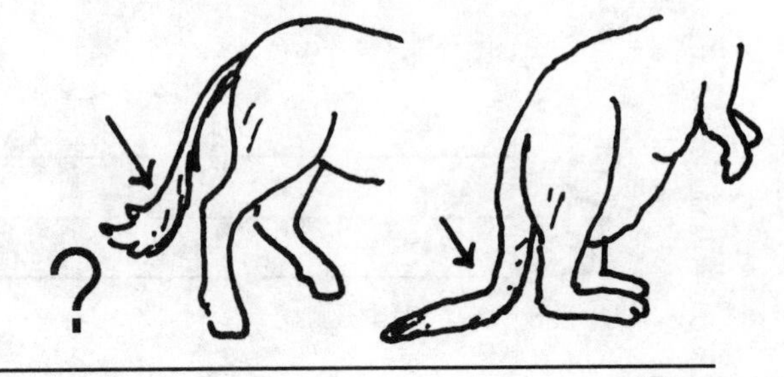
	2. necks ?	
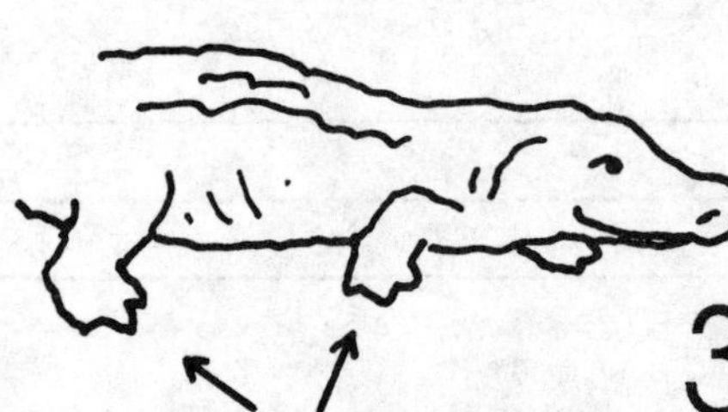	3. legs ?	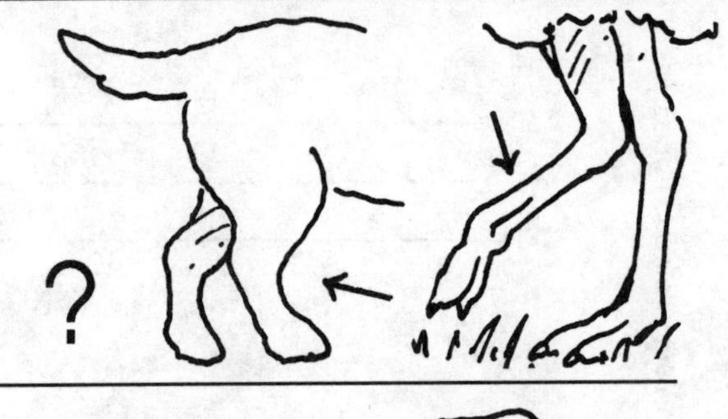
	4. noses ?	
	5. ears ?	

Name______________________________

97. Objective: To write the sentence pattern "(Rabbits) have (short) (tails.)" Procedure: Review the sentences about the animals made on the previous page. Say, "Write sentences about animals' bodies."

1. Rabbits have short tails.

2. ______________________________

3. ______________________________

4. ______________________________

5. ______________________________

6. ______________________________

98. Objective: To learn the names of special features that animals have. To reinforce question and sentence patterns: "What animals have (stripes)? (Tigers) have (stripes)." Procedure: Teach each of the body features. Ask, "What animals have stripes? (Zebras and tigers) What animals have spots? (Giraffes and leopards) (And so forth.) Color the pictures. Copy the words on another sheet of paper."

Name____________________________________

What animals have...

1. stripes ?	2. spots ?	3. trunks ?
4. feathers ?	5. wings ?	6. scales ?
7. beaks ?	8. shells ?	9. fins ?
10. claws ?	11. horns ?	12. antlers ?

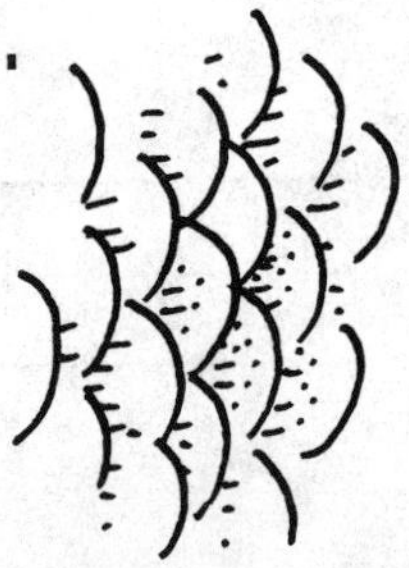

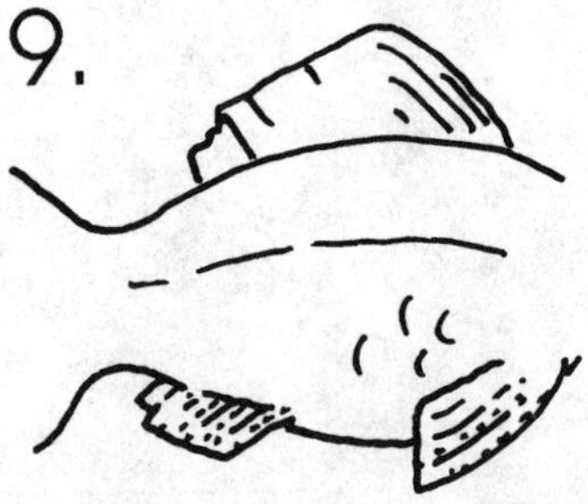

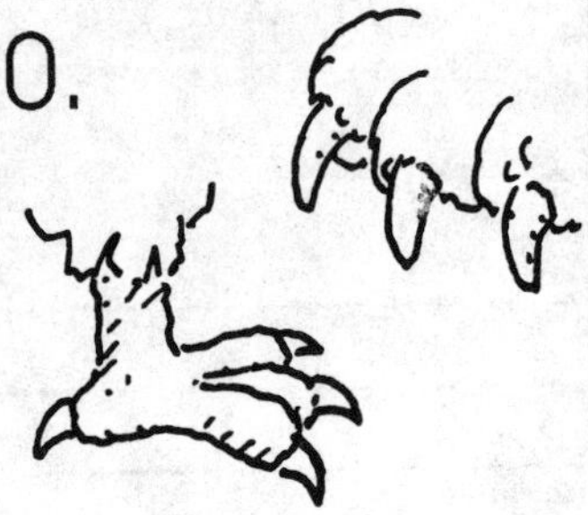

99. Objective: To write sentences with the verb have. Procedure: Say, "Read the sentence. Write other sentences about things animals have on their bodies."

Name____________________

1. Zebras and tigers have stripes.

2. ____________________

3. ____________________

4. ____________________

5. ____________________

6. ____________________

Name________________________________

100. Objective: To understand and read the question pattern: "Does a (rabbit) have a (tail)?" and the short answer patterns, "Yes, it does; no, it doesn't." Procedure: Read the title question. Teach the word blank. Point to the first word and make a question. "Does a rabbit have a tail?" Point to the two answers at the bottom of the page. "Yes, it does. Does a rabbit have wings?" Point to the other answer. "No, it doesn't." Make questions and student answers. Then say, "Now you make questions, and I will answer them."

Does a ________ have ________?

1. rabbit — a tail
2. zebra — feathers
3. bird — four legs
4. cow — long ears
5. chicken — stripes
6. cat — wings

☐ Yes, it does.

☐ No, it doesn't.

101. Objectives: To write questions using the pattern: "Does a (cow) have (wings)?" and answer those questions with a short answer form. Procedure: Read the words "does not" and "doesn't" in the box. Say, "Doesn't is the short way to say 'does not.'" Point to the first question. Say, "Read the question. Read the answer. Now you write questions about animals. Write the answers. You can write more questions and answers on another sheet of paper."

Name________________________________

Doesn't = does not

1. Does a cow have wings ?
No, it doesn't.

2. ________________________________

3. ________________________________

4. ________________________________

5. ________________________________

6. ________________________________

102. Objectives: To make sentences with the pattern: subject + verb + direct object; to understand and answer the question pattern, "What do (elephants) eat?" Procedure: Review the words for the animals and objects in the pictures. Then ask, "What do elephants eat? (Elephants eat) (grass and plants)." Ask questions about the other animals. The student may answer in a one-word or complete sentence answer. Say, "Color the pictures."

Name____

What do they eat ?

1. elephants	2. alligators	3. snakes
4. people	5. cows	6. birds
7. grass	8. fish	9. rabbits
10. insects	11. frogs	12.. plants

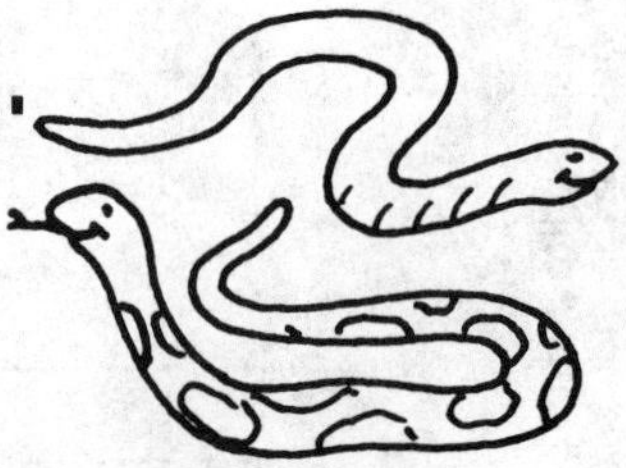

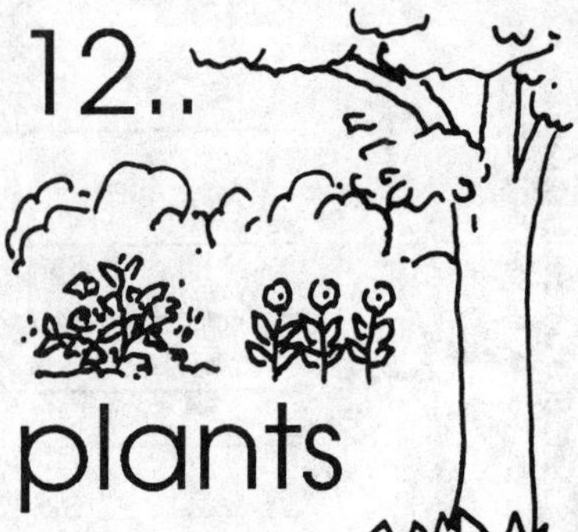

Name________________________________

103. Objective: To write complete sentences telling what animals eat. Procedure: Read the sentence at the top of the page. Say, "Look at page 102. Write sentences about what the animals eat."

1. Elephants eat grass and plants.

2. ________________________________

3. ________________________________

4. ________________________________

5. ________________________________

6. ________________________________

Name________________________________

can't =
can not

Can you . . .

1.

swim ?

☐ Yes, I can.

☐ No, I can't.

2.

run fast ?

☐ Yes, I can.

☐ No, I can't.

3.

climb a tree ?

☐ Yes, I can.

☐ No, I can't.

4.

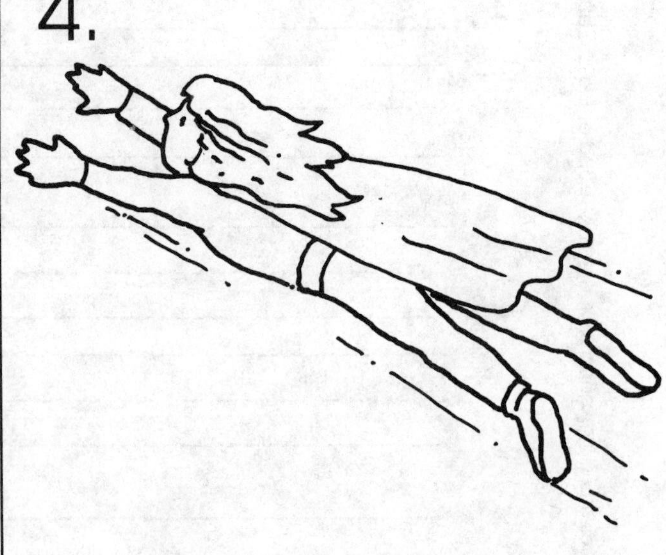

fly ?

☐ Yes, I can.

☐ No, I can't.

104. Objectives: To understand and respond to questions with "Can you + verb?"; to understand, use, and carefully pronounce the contraction can't; to use short answers, "Yes, I can; no, I can't;" new words: swim, fast, climb, fly. Procedure: Point to each picture and ask the question: "Can you (swim)?" Point to the answers. Say, "Check the correct answer." Then say, "Ask me the questions." Student asks you each question and you answer. Say, "Color the pictures. Copy the questions and answers on another sheet of paper."

Name____

I can ___________	I can not ________
______________________	______________________
______________________	______________________
______________________	______________________

105. Objectives: To increase verb vocabulary; to allow self expression; to reinforce the sentence patterns "I can / cannot + verb." Procedure: Say, "What can you do? Draw pictures here, under 'I can.' What are things you can not do? Draw pictures here, under 'I cannot.'" When the student has completed the pictures, teach the appropriate words and write them in each box. Say, "Tell me a sentence about each picture. Write sentences on another sheet of paper."

Name________________________________

1. Animals that can run fast.

2. Animals that can swim.

3. Animals that can fly.

2. Animals that can climb trees.

106. Objectives: To notice and categorize animal abilities; to reinforce verbs; to create sentences using the pattern "(Horses) can (run fast.)". Procedure: Read the title of each box. Say, "What animals can run fast? Write the animals here. What animals can swim? Write the animals here." (And so forth.) When the student has completed the page, say, "Make sentences about what the animals can do. For example 'Horses can run fast.' Write the sentences on another sheet of paper."

107. Objective: To learn additional verb vocabulary. Procedure: Read the sentences, saying "blank" where the student has to fill in the name of the animal. Then the student reads the sentences and tells the name of the animal. Say, "Write the name of the animal. Draw a picture of the animal. Copy the sentences on another sheet of paper."

Name ______________________________

1.

A ______________

lays eggs.

2.

A ______________

gives milk.

3.

A ______________

smells bad.

4.

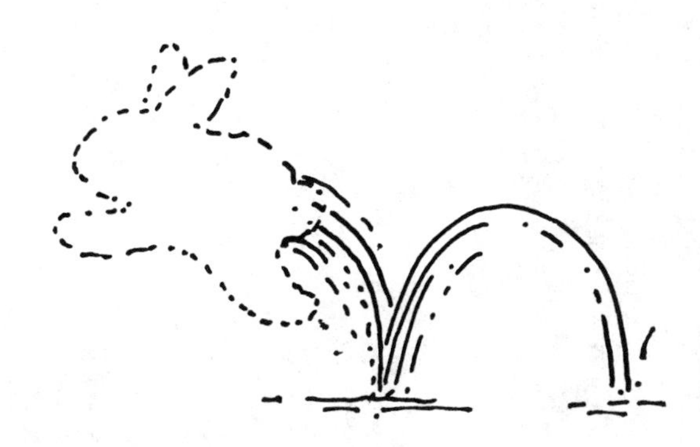

A ______________

can hop.

108. Objectives: To draw a picture of a favorite animal; new word: favorite. Procedure: Say, "I like monkeys. Monkeys are my favorite animal. What is your favorite animal? What animal do you like very much? Draw a picture of your favorite animal here. Write the word here."

Name________________________________

My favorite animal

1. This is my favorite animal.

2. It is a / an ______________________.

Name____________________________

1. My favorite animal is

a
an ____________________________.

2. It is ____________________ and

____________________________.

3. It has ____________________.

4. It lives ____________________.

5. It eats ____________________.

6. It can ____________________.

109. Objective: To write a short composition about a favorite animal; to reinforce the sentence patterns, adjectives and verbs that have been learned. Procedure: Say, "Read the sentences and complete them." The student orally completes the sentences as you listen and help. Then say, "Finish the sentences. You can look back at the other pages. Copy the story about your favorite animal on another sheet of paper." (Optional) "Read the story to the class (or to a group of other students.)" Hang up the picture and the story.

Name______________________________________

Write words and sentences.

110. Objective: Review. Procedure: Select words and sentences from previous pages to dictate to student. Assist if necessary with spelling. May be used to test or reinforce spelling.

111. Objectives: To write a short composition about oneself; to reinforce sentence patterns and vocabulary already learned. Procedure: Read the title and read the story, giving information about yourself. Say, "Now you read this and tell about yourself." When complete, say, "Write the sentences." Check the student's work and say, "Copy the story about yourself on another sheet of paper. Read the story about yourself to your friends (or to the class)." Hang up the student's work.

Name____________________________

All about me

1. I am a ____________________.

2. I am ____________________ and

____________________________.

3. I have ____________________.

4. I live ____________________.

5. I eat ____________________.

6. I can ____________________

____________________________.

GCIU
LOCAL 583